# SPEED SECRETS 4

# ENGINEERING
# THE DRIVER

D1554413

# ENGINEERING
# THE DRIVER

**ROSS BENTLEY**

**MOTORBOOKS**
INTERNATIONAL

This edition first published in 2005 by Motorbooks International, an imprint of MBI Publishing Company, Galtier Plaza, Suite 200, 380 Jackson Street, St. Paul, MN 55101-3885 USA

© Ross Bentley, 2005

All rights reserved. With the exception of quoting brief passages for the purposes of review, no part of this publication may be reproduced without prior written permission from the Publisher.

The information in this book is true and complete to the best of our knowledge. All recommendations are made without any guarantee on the part of the author or Publisher, who also disclaim any liability incurred in connection with the use of this data or specific details.

We recognize that some words, model names and designations, for example, mentioned herein are the property of the trademark holder. We use them for identification purposes only. This is not an official publication.

Motorbooks International titles are also available at discounts in bulk quantity for industrial or sales-promotional use. For details write to Special Sales Manager at Motorbooks International Wholesalers & Distributors, Galtier Plaza, Suite 200, 380 Jackson Street, St. Paul, MN 55101-3885 USA.

ISBN 0-7603-2160-4
**On the front cover:** *Courtesy Kent Regan*
**On the back cover:** *Courtesy Kent Regan*
Edited by Peter Bodensteiner
Designed by LeAnn Kuhlmann
Printed in the United States of America

# Contents

# Acknowledgments

This is the fourth book in the Speed Secrets line, so I've had the opportunity to thank many of the people who have had an impact on my racing knowledge. At least I can say that about the ones who have had an ongoing influence, for every day I learn more from the drivers I'm working with and our staff of Speed Secrets coaches. I continue to learn from my own racing experience, as well.

The first person I want to acknowledge here is a familiar name to you if you've read any of the other Speed Secrets books: Ronn Langford. Ronn continues to be a great friend and coach to me, and I recognize the fact that many of the concepts in this book began with him or were expanded through our working together. Thanks again, Ronn.

While I have learned a lot about racing through experience, what I've learned from racing seems to be far more important these days. In developing the Speed Secrets business (www.speed-secrets.com), everything I've learned through my years of racing has come in handy. Without those years in the racing business, we would not be anywhere near as successful, nor would this book be possible. Of course, it's what I've learned from the people I've met in this sport that really counts.

All the experience and knowledge in the world would not amount to anything without the opportunity to exploit it. For that, I thank Joe and Justin Pruskowski for believing in my dream to establish the very best driver development company in the world. Additionally, this business has as its foundation the books published by MBI, including this one. We really are "changing the way people drive."

And all the opportunities in the world will not make a dream a reality without great people. I have been lucky to have the encouragement of the talented staff at Speed Secrets, especially CEO Fred Wright and marketing genius Bruce Cleland. Without their expertise and hard work, I would not have had the time or energy to finish this book, nor the opportunity to continue to do what I do. Thanks to both of you.

Next to my family, Robin and Michelle, the people I'm most proud of are our *Speed Secrets* Coaching Team and our technical staff. When we say we provide "The Very Best Training. Period.", it's because of the talent and passion of these people. Thanks to all of you, and for your input and influence on this book.

And once again, thanks to Peter Bodensteiner and everyone at MBI for allowing me ramble on in print—and publishing it! It's so much easier to complete another *Speed Secrets* book when working with someone who has as much motorsport knowledge as Peter.

Finally, a lot of the prototyping of the techniques and concepts presented in this book came about while working alongside Jeff Braun. The first time he engineered a car I was driving, I realized he was a very special engineer. He understood so much more than just the technical aspects of the car. He understood the relationship between driver and car. Having Jeff write the foreword for the book is an honor. Thanks Jeff.

# Foreword

The modern race car is made up of a staggering number of sophisticated systems. Designers, race engineers, crew chiefs, and drivers constantly work to understand and tune these systems. Fortunately for people interested in gaining a better understanding of how these systems are optimized, there are many tools and resources available.

Carroll Smith wrote some great books about suspensions and vehicle dynamics. Wind tunnels allow engineers to make more downforce and less drag. Shock dynos have opened a whole new world of tuning race cars. Seven-post rigs bring the vehicle dynamics and shock absorber systems together, further increasing understanding. Tire testing methods have improved to the point where tires are less of a black art. Data acquisition systems have improved to the point where nothing goes unnoticed. Simulation software has allowed engineers to fine tune the race car before it even hits the track.

In the past 20 years I have had a chance to race-engineer cars for NASCAR champions, Sports Car world champions, F1 drivers, and many other world class drivers. At one time or another I believed each of the above areas of race car engineering was the most important to improving the performance of the car I was engineering for these drivers. It took me a while to figure it out, but I now realize that the system with the biggest influence by far on race car performance is the person steering it. Nothing on or in the modern race car is more complex, sophisticated, or technologically advanced—or more non-linear and less understood—than the driver.

I know of a major race car manufacturer that is spending huge amounts of time and money doing simulations and data studies to understand why the driver does the things he does in the car and how he perceives the limits of the car. They know that this area of engineering is the next step in car performance. The limit of the car matters not unless the driver can drive it there.

The book you hold in your hands will lay the groundwork for what I, and the smart car designers, believe to be the next major advancement in race car performance—engineering the driver.

I have had the good fortune of working directly with Ross for the past three seasons. I have seen his *Speed Secrets* driver-coaching techniques evolve to the point where the next step was to apply the same principles to the driver that I was applying to the race car. Ross describes how the driver and engineer can use these techniques to tap into hidden performance gains available within the driver.

It is nice to see someone finally take an engineering approach to race car drivers. We do such a good job analyzing, evaluating, predicting, and developing all other aspects of the race car, why not take the same approach with the most important aspect—the driver?

Thanks, Ross, for starting us all off in a new area of race car engineering. This is only the beginning, I'm sure.

—Jeff Braun
  October 2004

# Introduction

Early in the history of auto racing, particularly from the 1930s to the beginning of the 1960s, most of the emphasis in the quest for speed was put on developing more and more engine power; designers and engineers were in a never-ending competition for more horsepower. In the late 1950s and early 1960s, led by legendary engineers such as Colin Chapman of Lotus, the emphasis began to shift toward improving chassis and suspension design and tires. The 1970s and 1980s brought aerodynamic development. Since the 1990s, the emphasis has been on computers and electronic controls.

Not surprisingly during this time, little emphasis was placed on improving the driver's performance. It was typically assumed that a driver either had "it" or he didn't.

All that has changed. Over the past few years, more and more drivers and teams have discovered the value of improving the driver's performance. They have realized that there is more to be gained by "tuning" the driver than there is in the engine, chassis, suspension, tires, aerodynamics, computers, and electronics. The emphasis is now on engineering the driver—on maximizing his performance.

Certainly, development will continue on all the components of the car itself, but most of them have been fine-tuned to the point where there is now less to be gained than at the start of the technological learning curve. With the driver, however, there is much to be gained— the room for improvement is almost infinite. We are at the beginning of the driver performance learning curve.

Depending on the level or type of motorsport, hundreds, thousands, tens of thousands, hundreds of thousands, or millions of dollars—and countless hours—are spent on improving the performance of the car. But how much is spent improving the performance of the driver?

Typically, the job of improving the car's performance falls on the shoulders of the team's engineer, even if that person is also the team owner/manager, mechanic, friend/family member, or the driver himself.

11

At the most basic level, the engineer's job is to do whatever it takes to make the car perform more reliably, more consistently, and faster. Imagine doing the same with the driver: engineering him so that he performs more reliably, more consistently, and faster. That is what I mean by "engineering the driver"—doing whatever it takes to improve the performance of the driver. Think about it. An amazing amount of time and effort is spent on the car, when it can only ever be driven to its maximum by a driver performing at his best.

*Typically, the race engineer has focused strictly on making the car's performance better by tuning the suspension and aerodynamics. But increasingly more engineers, team managers, crew chiefs, and mechanics—at least the successful ones—are learning how to read the driver, work with the driver, and help maximize his performance.*

Whether it's SCCA club racing, Saturday night oval track, autocrossing, NASCAR, Indy car, or F1, every driver can be engineered to perform at a higher level. In fact, many teams already have a driver engineer . . . without knowing it. In this case, he or she is usually the car engineer, team owner, team manager, crew chief, mechanic, parent, friend, or spouse—in other words, anyone who can benefit from the driver improving and consistently performing at his peak. Unfortunately, most of these people do not know what it takes to engineer the driver.

I wrote this book for anyone who wishes to help the driver become a better driver, and/or wants him to drive as well as possible on a consistent basis.

I also hope there are drivers out there who will have the self-confidence, insight, and understanding to read this book themselves to learn self-coaching techniques; and then to pass it on to those around him who can help him—who can engineer him.

## SPEED SECRET #1
### The car will only perform as well as the driver who drives it.

How much time, money, and effort have you spent on understanding the race car—vehicle dynamics, mechanics, construction, aerodynamics, shock absorbers, and so on—in the past year alone? How much have you spent on understanding what your race driver goes through, what he is up against, and what will and will not result in him performing well? No matter what is done to the car, it will only perform at its best when the driver is performing his best.

My goal for this book is to help you, no matter what your relationship with the driver, to extract the ultimate performance out of him on a consistent basis. Armed with the knowledge, understanding, and strategies presented in this book, you can do that.

By the way, for the sake of simplicity only, I've used male pronouns when referring to the driver.

## Chapter 1

# Engineering the Driver

### Who Can Engineer the Driver?

Many people believe that unless you have driven a race car you cannot engineer or coach a race driver. They are wrong!

But how, you say, can you expect to help a driver if you have never raced? How can you relate to the race driver if you, yourself, have never been one? And how can you expect the driver to respect and accept your opinion and input if you haven't raced at his level?

Those are all good questions. And the answer to all of them is simple: You are not there to tell him how to drive. You are not there to show him how to drive. Your job is to help him perform at his maximum. This doesn't require that you have his driving abilities.

In fact, sometimes having superior knowledge, skills, and experience are hindrances. Why? Well, if your knowledge and experience are beyond that of the driver, you have lost your "beginner's mind." In other words, you may have forgotten what it is like to be at that level.

Am I saying that you must have less knowledge, skill, and experience? No, but I am saying that less knowledge, skill, and experience are not a problem. Having some experience behind the wheel of a race car will be beneficial, as you can sometimes understand or relate a little easier. But it is certainly not necessary.

In fact, one of the best things you could do for your driver if you have not driven a race car—or not driven one much—is to enroll in a racing school course. Gain some feel or refresh your memory for what it's really like out there. But please keep an open mind. After taking a driving school program, you are not an expert. Remember, "experts" make lousy driver engineers. They know too much—or, at least, think

*Anyone who could benefit from his driver performing better can learn to "engineer" him, from team members to parents—and even the driver himself. And you don't have to know more about driving to do so.*

they know too much. All you are trying to do by driving a race car is relate a little more, be more appreciative of what your driver is doing, be more empathetic to him—not get so that you can (or think you can) tell him what to do. That is not your role. Your role is to help him discover how to maximize his performance. Rarely does that involve you telling him how to do something.

This book is written with the understanding that you may have less driving knowledge, skill, and experience than the driver (although, if you have more, it will not hurt). It is meant to help you understand and relate to the driver by giving you the background on how a driver's mind works, how to communicate with him, and how to use practice and testing to "tune" the driver—how to "engineer the driver."

## Acceptance of Coaches and Driver Engineers

Who can engineer a race driver? You can. Probably the biggest challenge you face is in getting your driver to respect, accept, and want your assistance.

Ask your driver—or any serious race driver—if he is an athlete and I'm sure his response will be a resounding yes. Your driver may then go on to give you all the reasons why race drivers should be considered athletes, just as football, hockey, basketball, baseball, and tennis players, golfers, and track and field athletes are. He will point out all the physical and mental challenges he faces and compare them to other sports.

The one thing he will not mention, though, is that all other athletes have one thing that most drivers do not: a coach. Tiger Woods, perhaps the greatest golfer to ever live, had a coach (it's interesting to note that at the time of this writing, Woods had not won a major tournament since splitting with his coach in 2002). Michael Jordan based part of his decision to retire on whether or not Phil Jackson, one of the greatest coaches of all time, would continue to coach him. Carl Lewis, Wayne Gretzky, Martina Navratilova . . . you name the athlete, they all had or have coaches.

And yet, most race drivers do not have a coach. Why? As I see it, there are four main reasons:

1. Observing a race driver perform is more difficult than observing other athletes. Since the driver is hidden inside the car, it's a bit like a basketball coach only being able to see the ball go through or not through the hoop to determine if the player's shooting technique was correct. Or, a golf coach only being able to observe the ball landing on the green to determine if the golfer swung properly.

2. Since the cost of racing is so high, any "extra" expense is avoided.

3. Driving a race car is seen as a macho sport, and having someone "tell" you how to do it is not macho. For most people in motorsport, either the driver has "it" or he doesn't.

4. Particularly in the past, it has usually been easier to get a little more out of the car than the driver. With the level of sophistication and technology today, this is no longer the case.

One of your challenges, as I said, is to have your driver accept the concept of having someone—you—coach or engineer him. I would suggest starting by helping him understand that if he really wants to be considered an athlete, he needs a coach.

You might also point out that drivers at all levels of the sport, from Indy cars and F1 to sprint cars and NASCAR, are now seeing the benefits of coaching. He might be surprised at how many drivers have someone coaching them (even if that person is not referred to as a coach).

You should definitely make it clear to him that you have no intentions of telling him how to drive the car. Your sole objective is to help him do what he already knows how to do, just better. Your intentions are to help him bring out the best in himself, to help him fully extract all his natural talents.

You may have to ask him to keep an open mind to new ideas and concepts. In fact, you may ask him if the two of you can work together and explore a new approach to getting the most out of the both of you. After all, he will be helping you develop new skills just as much as you will be helping him—maybe even more.

### SPEED SECRET #2
### Engineering your driver does not mean telling him how to drive.

### Why Engineer the Driver?

So why should you engineer your driver? Whatever your role within the race team, engineering your driver can make you look good. There are countless examples of extremely talented race car engineers, mechanics, or team owners/managers who have never received the credit for what they have accomplished, simply because they have not had the driver who could take their equipment to the front. Without a driver performing at or near his peak, no matter what you do to the car, it is unlikely you will be as successful as you could be. Your reputation lies with your driver.

To be blunt, you could engineer and/or prepare the perfect race car, but without a driver performing at least as well as the car, you will not get the results you want.

Actually, you have two options if you want to win. The first option is to look really hard to find that one-in-a-million race driver who is going to go to the top no matter what and grab onto him (whatever that takes—even if it means adoption!). Unfortunately, finding that one driver can take a lot of time. The second option is do whatever it takes to turn your driver into that one-in-a-million.

There are many talented, skillful race drivers around. Few of them, however, access their full potential on a regular basis. They may show glimpses of brilliance, but these glimpses seem to occur more by accident than by intention. It is up to you, then, to help your driver access his skills and talent on a consistent basis, so that he can gain the advantage on the competition.

That is what engineering the driver is all about. But is it possible? Is it possible to turn any driver into someone special? I am not naive or stupid enough to think that just anyone can be the next world champion using the techniques and strategies presented in this book. However, I am also not naive and stupid enough to think that today's champions got to where they are now without any effort at all. In fact, few if any got to the top without a lot of work themselves, and the focused effort of someone else. That someone else can be you. And many champions used the exact techniques and strategies presented here.

There are times—many times—when a team will make the race car faster, only to have the driver drive it slower. Why is that? If the driver is not comfortable, and confident, he will never drive it anywhere near its potential. Never forget, a confident driver in a less-than-perfect race car will always be faster than an unconfident driver in a perfect race car.

Another reason for engineering your driver is to ensure that he never makes the same mistake twice, and that he never has to learn the same thing twice. In fact, that is one of the main roles of a driver engineer—to ensure that the driver learns from his experiences.

### SPEED SECRET #3
**The goal is to ensure your driver never makes the same mistake twice, or has to learn the same thing twice.**

The final but no less important reason for engineering the driver is financial. In almost all cases, more can be gained from the driver than from the car, and at a tiny fraction of the cost.

## Driver Development Stages

For most, the first step in becoming a race driver is attending a racing school, where skilled instructors teach them the basics. This is the teaching stage, where instructors (teachers) tell the students what they need to know to get on the track and begin gaining experience. For example, instructors teach the driver the ideal line for a corner, why he should use it, how to determine where it is, why and how to use reference points, how and when to downshift, and other basic skills and techniques.

The next step most drivers go through is instruction. At this stage, instructors correct and fine-tune the driver's basic techniques. Instructors tell the driver that he should use a later or earlier apex, brake later, begin accelerating earlier, and so on. Most drivers at this stage tend to instruct themselves as well, telling themselves what to do differently to make an improvement.

Very few drivers go beyond these two initial stages of formal race driving education. Most simply rely on experience—seat time—to further the learning process. Few ever receive any real coaching. Sure, some drivers continue to be instructed, even if this instruction is coming from someone who calls himself a coach, but it really is instructing. It is still based on correcting and fine-tuning driving technique—telling the driver what to do.

So what's the difference between instructing and coaching? Instructors continue to tell a driver what to do; coaches help drivers learn. Instructing is certainly good for one's job security; because often when you tell a person how to do something, you will continue to have to tell him how to do it, as he rarely truly learns from the experience. With coaching, the goal is to help the driver become aware of what needs improving, and how to go about making that change.

As an example, an instructor may tell a driver that he should apex a corner later or carry more speed into a turn, only to witness the driver make the same mistake over and over again. In most cases, the driver knows what he should do. The problem is that he doesn't know how to make the change—he doesn't know how to get his body to go along with what his mind is telling him. I think we have all been in that position at some time in our lives. We know we need to make a change, but we can't seem to find a way to do so. With race drivers, the classic example of this is knowing that a fast sweeping turn should be taken with the foot flat to the floor on the throttle, only to give a slight lift every time. It's as if the right foot has a mind of its own!

A coach either identifies the problem or assists the driver in identifying the problem himself, and then helps the driver develop a strategy to make that change. Often, that means tackling not only the physical act but also mental programming. Never forget that a driver's mind leads his physical technique.

The interesting thing is that an instructor usually requires at least as much knowledge or experience as the person he is instructing, while this knowledge is not necessary for a coach. The reason, as I said earlier, is that the objective for coaching is not to pass on information but to help the driver take what he knows and build on that information.

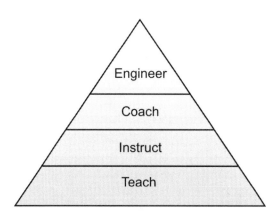

*In the beginning, a driver needs to be taught what to do. In the next level he needs instructing—fine-tuning and correcting of his skills and techniques. The third level is coaching, where a driver's abilities are drawn out, and the final level is driver engineering—doing whatever it takes to maximize the driver's performance.*

The final step in this process is, of course, driver engineering. Engineering the driver means doing whatever it takes to help a driver perform at his peak at all times.

The differences between coaching and engineering are:

• Coaching deals mostly with on-track activity, whereas engineering covers all aspects of a driver's career.

• Coaching deals mostly with physical technique, whereas engineering covers the physical and mental.

So can every race driver benefit from driver engineering? Can an elite level professional improve by use of the techniques presented in this book? How about an inexperienced or experienced club racer, oval track driver, vintage racer, or autocrosser? How about the young up-and-comer? In my experience, yes! I've personally engineered drivers at every one of these levels and have seen the positive results.

Actually, to be completely truthful, there is not one driver who cannot benefit from driver engineering: the driver who performs at his peak, who happens to be better than everyone else in the world, every time he is on the track. In other words, the perfect race driver. Unless that is your driver, then yes, he can benefit from driver engineering.

Now, the one assumption I'm making in this book is that the driver is beyond the beginner stage (having never driven any type of kart or car), otherwise he will not be ready for driver coaching or engineering. With little experience, that driver would best respond to *teaching* and/or *instructing*. If that is the case, he should spend a little more time in a good race driver development program, learning the basics. One of the roles of a driver engineer is determining the driver's level and getting him the necessary teaching and/or instructing if that is required.

## Performance

Typically, most people in racing look at performance from the perspective of the result. In other words, if the result is good, we think our performance was good; if the result was poor, we think our performance was poor.

Many times, though, a driver will drive the race of his life, but because the car was not quite up to the task, the result was a fifth or tenth place. Other times, a driver will win after making a number of errors—his personal performance was not great. Which of these are great performances?

The ironic thing is that when a driver focuses solely on getting a result, he rarely gets it; he gets too caught up in trying to get the result, in trying to go fast. When he focuses on his personal performance, on performing at his peak and the act of driving, he often gets the result he was after.

## SPEED SECRET #4
### Help your driver focus on his performance, and the results will look after themselves.

The goal of this book is to help you enhance your driver's performance and, therefore, ultimately get the result you both want. From all my talk about your driver's performance, I don't want you to get the idea that winning is not important. It is. It is why we compete. But the way to win is to perform better than the competition. That is what this book is all about: winning through maximizing the driver's performance.

# Chapter 2

# How the Driver's Mind Works

The physical act of driving a race car is relatively simple in comparison with the mental aspects. In other words, a driver's results are largely dependent upon his mental performance. Yogi Berra's comments about baseball could be adapted to racing as well: "Racing is 90 percent mental, and the other half is physical."

Since the goal of engineering the driver is to maximize his performance, having an understanding of how the driver's mind works is not only beneficial, it is critical.

In this chapter, I will give you a basic understanding of how your driver's mind works. Then, throughout the rest of the book, I will use this information to provide you with the specific tools to engineer your driver. The information in this chapter really is the foundation for much of the rest of the book. I should mention that all the information presented in this chapter is a review of the material Ronn Langford and I wrote about in *Speed Secrets 3: Inner Speed Secrets*. If you'd like a more in-depth understanding of the subject, please read that book.

My goal here is to give you enough information so that you will buy into the concepts and tools I want you to use; and so that you can provide the background knowledge to your driver so he will buy in. Without this basic understanding, I have my doubts whether you and/or your driver will believe in the concepts, and therefore, will use them. With this as a framework, let's dive into the driver's mind.

## The Performance Model

My friend and coach, Ronn Langford, developed the Performance Model to explain and understand how we, as humans, perform practically any activity. The model works like this: Information is input into our brains, which we can look at as operating like a computer. In this "bio-computer," the information is processed based upon our software or programming, resulting in an output. When it comes to driving a race car, this output is some form of action, reaction, or decision.

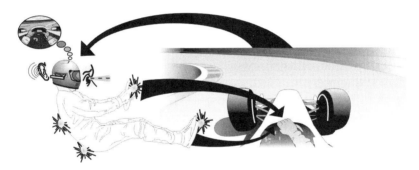

*Information from the driver's senses (visual, kinesthetic, and auditory) are input into his brain, which operates like a computer. Based on the software or programming in the brain, a psychomotor skill is triggered—an action. Then the loop begins all over again in reaction to the action.*

Anyone familiar with computers will know the term GIGO, which means garbage in—garbage out. The same thing applies to our minds: if we input garbage, the output will be garbage. Of course, the opposite is also true: quality in—quality out.

So where do race drivers get the information that is then input into the brain? From two main sources: sensory input and thoughts. Sensory inputs can be broken down further into visual, kinesthetic, and auditory.

Most information a driver puts into his brain when driving comes visually. What is not so obvious is what "visual" means. To many people, having 20/20 vision means having good visual input. While central vision acuity, which is what the 20/20 measurement relates to, is important, it is not the most important part of the visual input. For example, visual-spatial awareness, peripheral vision, depth perception, and the ability to change focal points rapidly are much more critical to race car driving.

## SPEED SECRET #5
### Improve your driver's sensory input and he will drive better.

This is exactly why some drivers with 20/20 vision do not "see" as much as others who have lesser vision.

The kinesthetic sense involves much more than just the sense of touch. It also includes a driver's proprioceptive system (the ability to sense forces acting against his body) and the vestibular system (the driver's sense of balance). Is a driver's sense of balance important to driving a race car? Is his ability to sense the g-forces against his body important? Is his ability to feel the vibrations and feedback through the steering wheel, pedals, and seat important? You bet!

Some people think that auditory input is not that important when it comes to driving race cars. Boy, are they wrong! A great driver receives

*A driver receives sensory input from visual, kinesthetic (feeling, motion, balance, and g-forces), and auditory sources. Improving the quality, and increasing the quantity, of sensory input for the brain will return better output—and the better the driver will drive.*

a lot of input from his hearing. He senses when the tires are at their limit of traction to a great extent by the sounds they make. He senses and sets his corner entry speed by the sound of the air rushing past his helmet or car. He uses the sound of the engine to tell him a lot about steering angle, shift points, traction, and so much more.

The overall message you should be getting from this is that anything your driver can do to improve the quantity and quality of sensory information going into his brain, the better his performance. One of the jobs of a driver engineer, therefore, is to help with this. I'll get into the details of how in Chapter 4.

## Driver's Software

You could have the latest and greatest super-computer, with the very best software or programming available, but if you give it poor quality or little quantity input, you will not get the output you were looking for. Conversely, if you give an old 386-processor computer lots of great quality input, you still will not get the output you were looking for. In other words, the processing speed of the driver's brain, and his software (programming), determines the output as well.

In fact, everything the driver does behind the wheel of the car—and outside of the car—is a result of the programming in his brain.

What do I mean by programming? Each and every time you do something, anything, the synapses in your brain that relate to that activity fire off bioelectrical current from one to another. This pathway now becomes the program for doing this act. The more often the act is completed, the deeper the programming becomes.

It is much like the pathway flowing water makes in dirt. The first time the water begins to flow, it seeks out a pathway. The more it flows, the deeper and stronger the pathway becomes. The same is true of the neural pathways in your brain. The more you practice anything, the stronger and deeper the programming becomes.

Let me make one thing very clear. A race car must be driven at the subconscious level, not the conscious level. Why? Because a race car is much too fast to be driven effectively at the conscious level. A driver cannot think through each skill and technique as he drives the car. If, at the end of a straightaway, he thought, "start braking now by moving my foot onto the brake pedal and squeezing it down, depress the clutch pedal with my left foot, move my right hand onto the shifter, move the shifter forward, blip the throttle . . . turn the steering wheel . . . ,"where do you think he would be? At best, at the back of the pack; but more realistically, crashed into a barrier.

### SPEED SECRET #6
### Driving must be a programmed or habitual act—
### something done without "thinking."

To emphasize the importance of driving at the subconscious level, consider this fact. A person's conscious mind processes information at a rate of 2,000 bits of data per second, while the subconscious mind processes at a rate of 4 billion bits of data per second! Is there any wonder why the subconscious is better at driving something as fast as a race car?

Your driver must rely on, and trust, his subconscious programming to drive the car. Where does that programming come from? Mostly from experience—physical programming. But it can come from mental programming as well. This is most often referred to as visualization or mental imagery.

Most drivers will tell you that they use visualization, when a majority of them really just close their eyes and think about what they want to achieve. Effective mental programming is more than just that. Mental imagery is really "actualization," where a person uses not only his visual sense but all his senses. He imagines not only what a scenario looks like, but also how it feels and how it sounds. The more senses he uses in his mental imagery, and the more real he can make it, the more effective a tool it will be.

In fact, mental imagery is, in many ways, a more effective way of programming one's brain than physical practice. Why? First and foremost, you don't practice making errors. Understand that every time a driver makes an error on the racetrack, he is getting better at making that specific error. After all, he just practiced it. The old saying, practice makes perfect, is not entirely accurate. Only perfect practice makes perfect. About the only time you do something perfect every time is when you imagine it.

Second, your mind does not know the difference between a real event and an imagined one. If you don't believe me, try this. Close your eyes, breathe slowly and deeply, and let yourself relax for three or four minutes. Then, picture in your mind a bright yellow lemon. Imagine picking up the lemon, feeling the texture of the skin, its ripples in the skin. Now see yourself taking a knife and cutting it in half, seeing and feeling the clear yellow juices running off

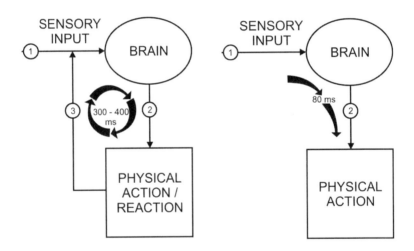

*In the illustration on the left: (1) The brain receives input from the senses. (2) Based on that information, a signal is sent to some specific muscles in the body to perform an action. (3) Feedback on how the action was executed, and the result of the action, is sent back to the brain where it is re-evaluated, reprocessed, and the loop begins again. Each loop requires 300 to 400 milliseconds to be executed. In the illustration on the right: With practice, the sensory input information will be recognized by the brain. Based on the recognized input, the brain will then send a "chunk" of signals to the muscles to perform a complete action. Therefore, the feedback loop is eliminated, meaning the action is executed more quickly and efficiently in as little as 80 milliseconds. This is why "perfect" practice—and the resultant mental programming—is so important.*

the knife blade and onto the table. In your mind, bring half of the lemon up to your nose and smell the lemon scent, then lick the juice off the surface.

What happened when you did this? If you're like most people and used your imagination well enough, your mouth began to produce saliva. Why? Because your mind didn't know the difference between a real lemon and an imagined one. This example demonstrates the power of our imagination to build our mental programming.

In addition to physical and mental programming, there is one other way that a driver develops the programming in his mind. This is external/internal programming, and it is often not very positive. For example, no matter how confident a driver is, if you were to tell him over and over again that he was not a good race driver, the programming of his belief system will change. He will lose the confidence that he once had.

It is amazing and sad how often this external programming occurs within a race team. I'm sure you can think of many examples of this programming in your own life. You can also imagine just how critical this is as it relates to your race driver and the team around him. Therefore, we will look at this in a bit more detail later.

### SPEED SECRET #7
### Everything, and everyone,
### affects your driver's programming.
### Use that to his and your advantage.

Internal programming can be just as destructive as external programming. I'm sure you have witnessed the person who mentally beats himself up over any and every little mistake. If a driver constantly says to himself, "I'm not very good in the rain," he's right, he will not be very good in the rain. The reason has nothing to do with his physical skills. It is just that he has programmed his mind, his belief system, that he is not good in the rain. The amazing thing about the brain is that it will fully live up to one's beliefs—positive or negative.

## Brain Integration

You are most likely aware of the fact that your driver's brain—and everyone else's, for that matter—is made up of two halves, or hemispheres. Each hemisphere has its own primary responsibilities: the left hemisphere for logic, math, language, and details; the right for creativity, intuition, art, the big picture.

How would you describe your driver? Is he a left-brain dominant person, meaning he is logical, factual, and detail-oriented? Or is he more right-brain dominant—creative, intuitive, and able to see the big picture?

Which do you suppose is the ideal for a race driver? If you answered "both" you are correct. A driver must be able to see the details and the big picture, be logical and creative, factual and intuitive. A driver must be "integrated," where both hemispheres of the brain work at their peak and work together.

In fact, sports researchers have shown that one of the most important factors that lead to an athlete performing "in the zone," or "in the flow," is having a fully integrated mind.

Between the two hemispheres of the brain is a bundle of nerve fibers called the corpus callosum. This acts as a communications link, transferring bioelectrical current between the hemispheres. But there is a dimmer switch effect in this communications link, one that can dial up or down the amount of bioelectrical communications between the hemispheres. When communications are restricted, the driver acts either more left-brained or more right-brained. When communications are turned up, the driver is integrated, which leads to great performances.

Also, the left hemisphere controls the right side of the body, and the right hemisphere the left side of the body. At least, that is the way it should be. Some people, and thus some race drivers—people often referred to as being uncoordinated—do not operate completely in this manner. Instead, their right hemisphere controls the right side of their body, and vice versa—at least partially.

When a person, your driver, becomes fully integrated, he will think more whole-brained and perform in a more coordinated fashion.

You can help your driver become more integrated. The exercises in Chapter 4 will help him improve his level of integration. My suggestion is that you do these exercises together, as they will help you in your role in the team as much as they help his performance behind the wheel.

## State of Mind

How important is your driver's state of mind to his level of performance? Critical, right? Unfortunately for most drivers, their state of mind is something that just happens, and they have little to no control over it. In other words, they either get into a great state of mind or not, and it is almost totally by accident. It is rare for a driver to have a defined process or ritual for triggering the ideal performance state of mind.

A driver's state of mind covers many areas: his level of anxiety, happiness, anger, nervousness, fear, passion, enthusiasm, empathy, and so on. As I'm sure you already know, these states of mind play a huge role in your driver's performance.

You can either hope that your driver shows up at each race in the right state of mind, or you can help him learn to trigger a performance state of mind. Chapter 4 describes a specific strategy to trigger that state of mind.

## Belief System

The single most limiting factor in a driver's performance is his belief system. What a driver believes about himself will have more of a bearing on his performance than anything else. The bottom line is, if your driver does not believe he is quick, he will not be quick.

I've sometimes wondered if a driver's belief system can be so strong that it can overpower the laws of physics. When you see some of the feats that Ayrton Senna performed with a car, you can't help but wonder where the *real* laws of physics are. If you witnessed his drive at the 1993 European Grand Prix at Donington in the rain, where he simply drove past others cars in the corners by carrying what looked like 5 or 10 miles per hour more, you know what I'm talking about. In case you missed it, he started fifth, passed Michael Schumacher, Karl Wendlinger, Damon Hill, and Alain Prost on the first lap, and went on to a victory that is part of Grand Prix racing folklore. Physics told me, and everyone else watching, that he couldn't do that—that he was driving beyond the limit. It was obvious that no one bothered to tell Senna.

Perhaps, it is not that Senna's belief system overpowered the laws of physics—that he was driving beyond the laws of physics—it is just that we do not know or understand all the laws yet. That is, of course, a fact. We do not know all there is to know. Anyone who thinks we do is missing the boat.

Sometimes, being a little ignorant can be a good thing. Knowledge can sometimes lead to limitations. If your driver believes the limit of the car is at some specific point, or certain lap time, what are the chances of him ever exceeding that? Slim to none.

Our world, especially the world of sports, has countless examples of this. At one time, scientists, researchers and, therefore, athletes thought that if someone were to run the mile in less than four minutes, they would practically drop dead. Then along came Roger Bannister in 1954, who didn't believe these "laws of physics," and who ran the first sub-four-minute mile. Within the following twelve months, four other runners ran a sub-four-minute mile—a limit that for decades had seemed impossible. Once armed with the knowledge—with the belief—that it could be done, it was relatively easy.

Watching Michael Schumacher or Juan Montoya, you can't help but be impressed with more than their skills. It is the strength of their belief system, on a consistent basis, that is most impressive. That is what makes them as successful as they are.

Where do a driver's beliefs come from? They are programmed into his subconscious in three different ways:

1. Physically/Experiential: When your driver experiences being quick, his belief system is programmed to believe he is quick. If he is not quick, he will form a belief that he is not quick. This is how most of a driver's belief system is developed.

2. Mentally: Your driver can affect his beliefs about being quick by pre-playing being quick in his mind, using mental imagery.

3. Externally/Internally: You, and other people, can have a great effect on his belief system. If you were to continually tell him that he is quick, over a period of time he will begin to believe that he is quick. Of course,

the opposite is also true. And his self-talk can also affect his beliefs. If he keeps telling himself that he is quick, it will have some effect.

If most of your driver's programming of his beliefs came about from past experiences, how can he begin to believe he is quick before he goes quick? It's a chicken and egg situation. Which comes first, the belief of being quick, or actually being quick, which results in the belief of being quick? Of course, there is no definitive answer to that question.

Often, a driver's beliefs about his abilities and his quickness come before he ever sets foot in a race car. If he has been successful in other areas of his life, particularly other sports, he begins to believe that he is good at everything. The more success he has had in other areas, the stronger his beliefs.

The good news is that your driver can change his beliefs about himself.

## SPEED SECRET #8
### The driver's beliefs about himself are the biggest limitations to his performance—and you can influence those beliefs.

The first step in your driver changing his belief system is becoming aware of his beliefs. He should make a list of his positive and negative beliefs, being totally honest with himself. The list should include what he believes about himself from the physical technique aspect and the mental side. He does not need to share the list with you or anyone else. This is for him to become more aware of himself. After all, if he doesn't know what to change, how is he going to change it?

Once he is honestly aware of his beliefs, he can choose to reprogram any negative ones. Changing negative beliefs rarely happens overnight. It usually requires a driver doing a couple of mental imagery sessions per day, backing that up with some physical signs of improvement, more mental programming, more physical evidence and programming, and so on. Without the mental programming, it is unlikely his beliefs will ever change—unless, by some fluke, he happens to go quick, in which case he will have experienced it.

You've probably witnessed this many times. A driver who seems to have what it takes to win keeps finding ways to lose—either he makes a mistake near the end of the race or the car breaks. Then, practically out of the blue—by fluke—everyone in front of him breaks, he wins, and then look out! He begins to win everything in sight. What was the difference? Did he gain a bunch of driving talent all of a sudden? No, just one thing changed: his belief system.

## Decision Making

Your driver's decisions in the race car cannot be made at the conscious level. If they are, he will make a lot of bad decisions. The reason, of course, is there is not enough time to make them at the conscious level. They must just happen at the subconscious level.

Remember the information I presented earlier about how quickly your driver's brain processes information—2,000 bits of information per second at the conscious level; 4 billion bits of information per second at the subconscious level. Any wonder why decisions, and just about everything else done in a race car should be accomplished at the subconscious level?

If you consider what it takes to make a good investment decision, one of the keys is having as much quality information as possible. The more, and the higher the quality, the better. Sound familiar? Many bad decisions race drivers make are a result of a lack of quality information. Where does that information come from? Visually, kinesthetically, and auditorily—sensory input.


### SPEED SECRET #9
### The more quality information your driver has, the better his on-track decisions will be.


If your driver can increase the amount and improve the quality of the sensory input heading into his brain, he will make better decisions on the racetrack. Fortunately, that can be done. The details are in Chapter 4.

## Focus

As you read this sentence, do not think about a pink elephant. I said, do not think about a pink elephant! So what are you thinking about? A pink elephant, right? In fact, it is impossible to not *not* think about something. The only way your driver cannot think or focus on something he doesn't want is to think or focus on something he does want.

For example, I have had the unenviable experience of coaching a driver who had a crew chief who would often say something along the lines of, "don't crash the car this time," or "don't worry, if you crash I can fix the car." He would say this to him just before driving out of pit lane! Now, I know that this seems like an extreme example, but this happens more than you can imagine. In this case, what do you suppose the driver's brain was focused on? Crashing, right?

Obviously, it would be ideal if everyone around your driver could be aware that what they say can affect his performance, but that is not always practical. So your driver must have a plan or strategy to manage whatever anyone says or does.

In the case of not *not* thinking about something someone says, the strategy is fairly simple. To demonstrate, imagine a blue elephant. Whenever anyone says "pink elephant," imagine a blue elephant. What you have done is developed a preplanned thought. Now, when I say, "don't think about a pink elephant," what do you think about? I hope you thought of a blue elephant. If you didn't, you need to practice this some more.

### SPEED SECRET #10
### *Provide your driver with something to focus on.*

The point is your driver must have a preplanned thought ready and willing to take on any unwanted thoughts thrown at him by you or anyone else, intentionally or not. Ask your driver to develop one, to let you know what it is, and practice using it. Perhaps his preplanned thought could be similar to mine. I use "car dancing." Whenever anyone says anything that could distract my focus, or get me focusing on something I don't want, I simply say "car dancing" to myself. When I say that phrase, I immediately conjure up an image of driving a race car at the limit on a wet track (which I just happen to love doing). Through years of practice, this image is a very strong and vivid one for me, one that will take the place of practically anything anyone says or does.

By the way, the more meaning the preplanned thought has for your driver, the more it will be effective. That is why "car dancing" works so well for me, but may not for your driver. To me, "car dancing" provides me with the image of me and the car smoothly and precisely flowing through the turns on a racetrack—dancing with the car.

This same theory can be applied to where your driver looks when he is driving. Particularly if he is driving on an oval or street course track, thinking to himself (or you telling him) not to look or think about the walls lining the track will not do any good. When he says, "don't think about the walls" to himself, his mind only really registers the "walls" part of the message. And the amazing thing about the mind is that if you put an image or thought into it, it will find some way of making it happen—even if that means driving into the wall.

So instead of thinking, "don't look at the wall," your driver should think, "look at the line I want the car to follow." The only way of *not* thinking or looking at what he *doesn't* want to think or look at is to think or look at what he *does* want. I know that is a mouthful, but it is completely true. Go back and read it again.

### Personality Traits

They say you should treat everyone as equals. I disagree. The reason I disagree is that everyone is not the same. Now, I know what is meant by the saying, and actually I do agree that everyone has the same potential. However, everyone is different, and therefore should be communicated with and managed differently. The reason is that everyone has different personality traits.

There are a number of personality trait profiling methods, the most popular ones being PDP (Professional DynaMetric Programs), Performax, and Meyers-Briggs. Each has been used and fine-tuned by millions of people, making them extremely accurate in providing an individual's personality profile. Although each method may use a slightly different set of traits, all provide a similar result.

When it comes to race drivers, one of the most useful personality trait profiling methods breaks the person's personality into four categories:

- Dominance: The measure of how dominant a person is or isn't, on a scale from not very dominant to very dominant.
- Extroversion: The measure of how outgoing, or how much of a "people person" someone is, from being very introverted to very extroverted.
- Pace/Patience: The measure of what pace a person prefers to work at, or how patient he is, from very impatient to very patient.
- Conformity: The measure of how one conforms to doing things "by the book." In the case of race drivers, this relates more to whether the person tends to follow the "rules," or how detail-oriented they are—from not very detail-oriented to very detail-oriented.

As an exercise, ask yourself where on each scale you want your driver. Do you want him to be very dominant, or not so? Do you want him to be extroverted or introverted? Patient or impatient? Do you want him to be detail-oriented or not?

What are the advantages and disadvantages of each? If he is very dominant—especially if he is also low on the patience scale—he may crash a lot since he will tend to be very aggressive and try to force his position. On the other hand, if he is not dominant enough, he may not win many races since he will tend to let other drivers push him around. You may want your driver to be extroverted to make him loved by the media and provide the maximum exposure for your sponsors. But one of the traits of a very extroverted person is that they love to be loved, and hate to be hated. If he is too extroverted, he may be a little too nice to his competitors on the track, in fear that they will not like him.

Obviously, if your driver is too patient he will not win often, and if he is not patient enough he will crash too often. And what about his level of attention to detail? If he is not detail-oriented at all, he will not make a good test driver, nor will he be consistent. However, if he pays too much attention to the details, he will most likely be slow. Some drivers are concerned about making sure every line they drive through a corner is perfect within a fraction of an inch, even if that means scrubbing off speed.

Actually, the perfect race driver is one who can adapt, one who can be dominant one second and less dominant the next—when the time is right to close the door on the competition and show who's boss, or to back off and wait for a better opportunity. The perfect race driver can be extroverted when it is time for the media and sponsors, and introverted and self-centered when behind the wheel. He is patient when the situation suggests that would be best, and has a sense of urgency when that is needed. He also pays attention to details to a certain point, and knows when to let go of them and get on with the job at hand.

You see, the perfect race driver is like a chameleon. He adapts to the situation. If you look at the real great champions, you see that they did that. Was Rick Mears dominant or not? Was he extroverted or not? Was he patient or not? Was he detail-oriented or not? How about Ayrton Senna? Al Unser Jr.? Dale Earnhardt? Michael Schumacher? Juan Pablo Montoya?

In fact, Earnhardt may have learned to adapt better than anyone. At one time, early in his career, he was simply dominant, introverted, and impatient. With experience he learned to adapt. He learned to dial down his level of dominance, turn up his extroversion (when it was time for a media interview or sponsor function), and dial up his patience. That is one of the reasons he was the great driver that he was. He could adapt his personality to suit the situation.

Your driver must learn to do the same. Chapter 4 discusses using mental imagery or visualization to change your driver's mental programming, which is where his personality traits lie. They are part of his programming. However, his programming can be changed. In fact, his programming can be that his programming can change. In other words, part of his programming can be that he can adapt his personality traits. If he imagines having four knobs on his chest, one marked D (for Dominance), one E (Extroversion), one P (Pace/Patience), and one C (Conformity), then he can imagine cranking each up or down depending on the situation—if the situation requires being more dominant, he just reaches up and cranks up his D. Or, if the situation dictates being more extroverted, he dials up the E, and so on.

For many drivers, learning to adapt their personality traits is the key to being a champion race driver. This only occurs as a result of reprogramming by way of mental imagery.

# Chapter 3

# *How Drivers Learn*

If you had to choose just one thing that separated the real superstars of any sport from the rest, what would it be? Superior eye-hand coordination? Desire to win? Work ethic? Natural talent?

While all these traits, and many more, are factors, the one thing that truly separates the greats from the not-so-greats is the ability to learn. In my opinion, the superstars of any sport are not necessarily born with any more natural talent than anyone else. It is what they do with that natural talent that really makes them great.

Rather than assuming your driver has just so much talent in his mind/body, and all you can do is hope it all comes out when driving your car, why not help him to learn more, to develop his talents? This chapter is all about learning how drivers learn. With that knowledge, you will be better equipped to help him develop. You will be better at engineering him.

## Learning Styles

Every person who learns anything (and that includes race drivers!), learns in a different way. We all have our own preferred, or dominant, learning style. Some drivers learn better when things are presented or approached visually, others auditorily, and others learn best when they experience things—a kinesthetic style.

The main point is that if your driver's preferred learning style is kinesthetic, and you proceed to *tell* him how to do something, don't blame him if he doesn't get it. If his preferred learning style is auditory, and you use a picture to illustrate something to him, you are the one to blame for him not understanding it. If you want someone to learn something, present it to that person using his preferred learning style. If not, he may have a difficult time learning it.

So how do you know what your driver's preferred learning style is? Observe him when he has really learned something quickly and effectively, and relate that to how it was presented to him. The easiest way, however, is to ask him. And if he doesn't know? Ask him to think back to when he learned something in his life quickly and easily—how was it presented? Was it told to him (auditory)? Was it shown to him (visual)? Or did he have to experience it (kinesthetic)? Armed with that information, experiment with the different styles to see which is most effective.

Having said that, the most effective way of learning is to combine all three learning styles at one time. Use the preferred style, and back it up with the other two. For example, to have him truly learn the apex of turn two, tell him where other drivers apex, draw him a picture of its location, and physically drive him or walk him through the corner.

## Learning Stages

Whether it is learning to walk, throw a ball, or drive a race car, all human beings go through four learning stages:

1. Unconscious Incompetence
2. Conscious Incompetence
3. Conscious Competence
4. Unconscious Competence

It may be easiest to relate these four stages to a baby learning to walk. In the beginning, a baby is at the *unconscious incompetence* stage—he hasn't yet discovered that people can walk. In other words, he doesn't know what he doesn't know how to do.

At the *conscious incompetence* stage, the baby has seen his parents walking and wants to, but can't. This is a case where he knows what he doesn't know how to do.

The next stage, the *conscious competence*, is where the child has to think about each and every step. He knows what to do, but he's having to do it at the conscious level.

44

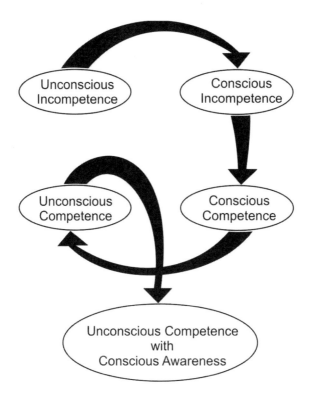

*With every skill and technique a driver learns he goes through Learning Stages. The Conscious Competence stage is where the driver has to consciously think about everything; the Unconscious Competence stage is where the driver does it without thinking— driving at the auto-pilot or subconscious level. But without the fifth stage—Conscious Awareness—the likelihood of the driver improving is low. Driving at the subconscious level while being aware at the conscious level (Unconscious Competence with Conscious Awareness) is practically the definition of being "in the zone."*

Finally, at the *unconscious competence* stage, the toddler no longer has to think about walking; it now happens automatically—he just does it. He doesn't think about what he knows. He knows and does—and doesn't have to think about it.

Every driver goes through each of these four stages with every technique he learns. As an example, blipping the throttle while downshifting. At one point, your driver didn't know the technique existed, knew nothing about it, and knew nothing about why a driver does it (unconscious incompetence). Then he became aware of the technique, but didn't know how to do it (conscious incompetence). As he began to practice it, he had to think through each detail (conscious competence). Finally, after practicing it over and over, it became automatic—a habit—and he no longer had to think about it, he just did it (unconscious competence). Obviously, to drive a race car quickly, your driver must reach this last stage. This is driving at the subconscious level.

This information, these stages of learning, can be found in most textbooks on learning strategies. I would, however, like to add a fifth stage that is not included in the textbooks, but that I have witnessed and experienced at the racetrack. At least when it comes to driving race cars, and I believe with most everything else, there should be an *unconscious competence with conscious awareness* stage.

The unconscious competence stage is much like the experience of driving somewhere, only to get there and not remember actually driving there. I'm sure you have experienced that at least once in your life. You are driving completely on auto-pilot; your mental programming is handling the chore, while your conscious mind is off in another world.

Yes, at this level you are operating about as efficiently as possible, but you are *unaware*. Think of it this way. You've been driving the same route to work for years. You drive to work but don't remember doing it. You are certainly competent at it, so much so that you didn't even have to consciously think about it. However, while your conscious mind was off in another world, the highway construction crew built a new road—a shortcut—that would cut your commute time in half. Because your conscious mind was unaware, though, you never noticed.

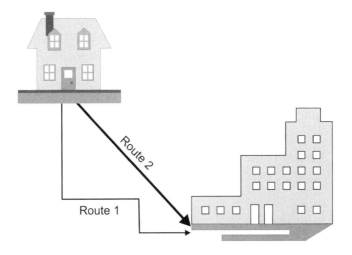

*Have you ever driven from your home to work, and upon arriving, realized you don't remember driving there? Most people have. That's illustrated by Route 1 above, and it's what happens when you operate only at the Unconscious Competence stage. You're doing it very well, but the chances of doing it better are slim. Without Conscious Awareness you are likely to be unaware of a new super-highway, Route 2, having been built. It's when you're at the Unconscious Competence with Conscious Awareness stage that you perform at your peak, and continue to improve.*

Unless your conscious mind is aware, you will never make any improvements. Yes, you will continue to drive very well at the subconscious, programmed level, but you will never upgrade the performance of that programming. Many times, this is the reason for a plateau on the learning curve—a complete unawareness of what could or should be improved.

### SPEED SECRET #11
### *Awareness is the key to improving*

The ultimate goal for any race driver is to drive at the subconscious level, relying and trusting his programming, while using his conscious mind to observe and be aware of any ways to improve the programming. It should be as if the conscious mind is looking over the driver's shoulder, much like an in-car camera would see it, watching for opportunities to upgrade the software.

## The Learning Formula

Perhaps the single most important piece of information in this book is this: MI + A = G. What does this mean? It is the secret to learning, the key to improving, the holy grail of making changes—the learning formula. That's all.

In this equation, MI represents Mental Image, A represents Awareness, and G is the Goal. The amazing thing is that if your driver has a clear mental image of what he wants to achieve, and an awareness of where he is right now, his mind will do what is necessary to make the two match, resulting in the goal. It is the most natural and efficient way of learning something new or making a change in technique.

When I first discovered and began using this learning technique, my abilities as a driver engineer improved tenfold. As an example, let's say your driver is consistently over-slowing the car entering a particular corner. You could just tell him over and over again to "carry more speed into the turn." Will that work? Not likely. You could ask him to do some mental imagery—visualizing or mental programming—of braking a little lighter, not taking as much speed off, and entering the turn 2 or 3 miles per hour quicker. Will that work? Most likely, but it will take awhile.

The reason it could take some time to take effect is that he may *only* have the mental image of what he wants to do. He may not have any awareness of what speed he is currently carrying into the turn. So ask him to rate his corner entry speed on a scale of 1 to 10, with 10 being the ragged edge, the limit, ten-tenths. Then, send him onto the track and ask him to tell you over the radio how close to a 10 he is each lap—how close is he to the mental image of his goal? By combining the mental image with awareness, he will begin to carry more speed into the corner before you know it.

## SPEED SECRET #12
### If your driver is unable to do something, he's missing either mental image or awareness.

Again, if a driver has a clear mental image, and an awareness of what he is doing right now, his mind will bring the two together. You may be surprised at how rare it is for drivers to have both of these components. Some may have a clear mental image of what they want to accomplish, but have no awareness of what they are currently doing. Others do not have a mental image of what they want, mostly because they are overly aware of what they are currently doing—they are so focused on what they are doing wrong, they can't get the mental image of what they want.

### Learning from the Inside Out

Drivers, and everyone else in the world, learn in one of two ways: from the inside out or from the outside in.

Learning from the outside in is what most people typically think of as learning. This is how we were taught in school. Learning from the outside in is what happens when you "teach" your driver something. It is the definition of you telling him what to do, or of giving him information. It is the information or knowledge coming from the outside (from you), and getting in him.

Actually, the getting in is not much of a problem; it is the staying in that is the challenge. And, without staying in, he really hasn't learned it.

On the other hand, learning from the inside out is what coaching and driver engineering is all about. Learning from the inside out is when your driver discovers or learns something for himself—often through your guidance or stimulation—rather than just being told what to do.

As an example, in the past I have spent countless hours teaching drivers about the line through various corners. I have talked to them about the turn-in point, the apex, the exit, and why it all matters. I've discussed the reasoning behind the line until I'm blue in the face. And yet, many times the drivers I'm talking to do not drive the line consistently (if at all).

Of course, what I've been doing is attempting to have them learn from the outside in. It has only been in the past few years that I've learned myself just how effective and efficient learning from the inside out really is. Recently, when trying to get a driver to understand why one specific line through the corner is more effective than another (or no line at all!), I took an entirely different—and unique—approach. Instead of telling him where he needed to drive, I used a tool (I'll share that with you soon) that helped him become aware of what the car needed, and let him discover (learn) for himself where the line is. His

*The goal of engineering your driver is not to tell him how to do things, but to help draw out what he already knows. He may or may not know this at a very advanced or detailed level, but when it is drawn out of him, he will have truly learned it—not just memorized the information told to him.* Bruce Cleland comment after using this tool was, "Oh, that's why you wanted me to drive that line!"

This type of learning is so much faster, efficient, and long-lasting. In fact, once a driver learns from the inside out where the line is, he will know it forever. He will also be able to apply it in other corners, at other tracks, and with other techniques.

If you have ever wondered why some drivers seem to have a knack for knowing "instinctively" where the line is for a corner, while others struggle with it or need to be told by someone, this is the reason. Once a driver truly understands *why* the car needs to be driven on a certain line through a corner, he will have learned the feel for it, and will be able to apply that to each and every corner he faces.

## SPEED SECRET #13
### Draw the answer out of your driver, rather than drill it into him.

Of course, this approach works equally well for all aspects of driving, not just learning the cornering line. You can tell your driver to carry more speed through a corner, be smoother with his downshifts, or turn the steering wheel more progressively, but as long as you are telling him how or what to do, he will not fully learn it.

You may have recognized a great side benefit of this approach to learning. You do not have to know more about the subject than your driver. All you need to do is find the key to raising his awareness of the core reason and/or function of the technique. That may sound like a difficult task, but when you begin using the driver engineering tools presented in Chapter 4, it will become much easier than you thought.

### Trial and Error
Is there anything wrong with your driver making an error? I know, I know, it depends on how much the error costs and who's paying for it. But if you want your driver to improve, or even just to perform at his

very best right now, you and he must be willing to have him make a few errors. Why? Because, looked at and used in the right manner, errors are a valuable learning experience.

If you think about it, when we were young, trial and error was our most common and effective learning technique. Take the act of learning to walk, for example. Imagine if, after falling down the first few time you tried to walk, your parents said, "We don't want you trying that any more—you always seem to fall down." Or you, yourself, thinking, "I can't seem to get this right, so I think I won't bother trying any more."

Pretty absurd, right? And yet, we do this with race drivers all the time. The second they make a mistake, we let them know in some way (sometimes subtle, sometimes not so subtle) to never make that error again. And, how often does that help? Not very often!

Of course, crashing a race car is much more expensive than the damage caused when you fell down while learning to walk. The point is, though, the more you resist errors, the more your driver resists errors, and the more likely it is for him to make more.

One of the biggest differences between great drivers and not-so-great drivers is *not* that the former makes fewer errors. In fact, they both make about the same number of mistakes. The difference is that the great drivers recover from, learn from, and know how to minimize the consequences of most errors. That only occurs when there is an atmosphere that allows errors, and allows learning from them.

Errors are simply a form of feedback that helps a driver hone in on the desired goal. They are signals that help the driver continue to improve.

### Learning Through Osmosis

Why do you think second-generation drivers such as Michael Andretti and Al Unser Jr. were so good (and why their third-generation sons are so good)? Is it because of their genes, what they inherited from their fathers? While I won't say their fathers had nothing to do with their abilities behind the wheel, I don't believe their driving had much, if anything, to do with their DNA. But I do think they acquired most of their "natural talent" from their fathers prior to ever getting in a race car.

Michael Andretti and Al Unser Jr. acquired much of their talent by keenly observing their fathers, by absorbing everything they were exposed to as children. And in both cases, that was a lot to absorb. They learned through osmosis.

All race drivers learn through osmosis. The more they are exposed to, the more they learn.

Tennis coaches in England have noticed for years a direct correlation between their students' abilities and the television coverage of Wimbledon. For a couple of weeks immediately following the tournament, tennis players' performances improve significantly. Did they practice more, change their swing, or buy a new tennis racket? No. They simply learned by watching.

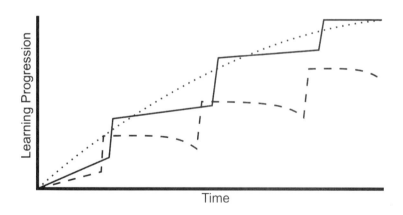

*In* Speed Secrets 2 *I introduced the idea of Learning Steps (the solid line) as opposed to the commonly defined learning curve. There's an all-too-common variation—the Frustration Steps (dashed line). This is where a driver, frustrated by the lack of improvement (a plateau), begins to try too hard and actually gets worse. It's only when the driver gives up and relaxes that he begins to improve again.*

Your driver can learn a lot by watching other drivers. Of course, it makes sense that he should observe and learn from the best he possibly can. He will not learn as much from watching drivers who are not as good as he is, although it is still possible to get something from that experience.

## Learning Progression

Every driver, no matter how much natural talent you think he has or doesn't have, will continue to improve throughout his career. Even drivers reaching the ends of their professional driving careers still improve in some areas (which, unfortunately, are often overcome by other factors, such as lack of motivation or desire, or a deterioration of physiological functions). How quickly, and how consistently, they improve all depends on the person and his environment.

One thing is clear, though. No two drivers have ever—or ever will—progress at the same rate. Some drivers' learning curve is mostly a steady upward incline, while others are full of steps of all shapes and sizes.

What is very common is for a driver to plateau. Often, the driver and the people working with him become frustrated with the lack of progress, and the plateau lasts longer. In my experience, most plateaus are followed by a sharp incline in progress—if the frustration is controlled and if there is a focus put toward improving the driver's awareness.

Many times the plateaus appear to be steps backward. It is like one step back, two or three forward, one step back, two or three forward, and so on. I like to compare them to the calm before the storm. In this case the calm is the apparent lack of progress, and the storm is the whirlwind of learning.

## SPEED SECRET #14
### *A learning plateau is the sign of an opportunity for improvement.*

If you think back to the learning stages, you understand why. Most often, for a driver to progress, he must go back to the conscious competence stage, where he thinks through each step in a mechanical manner. This results in too much conscious thought, and an apparent step backward. If the driver doesn't become frustrated and has a little patience, this new technique, skill, or mental approach becomes part of his programming. He then progresses to the unconscious competence stage, where it becomes something that he seems to do naturally. At this point, there is a significant step up in the learning process.

# Chapter 4

# Driver Engineering

### Driver Engineer's Toolbox

With the information from the previous chapters in mind, let's begin to define some practical and specific methods of engineering your driver. While using these methods, you may have to go back and review how your driver's mind works, and how it learns. It is critical, for example, to know about and use your driver's preferred learning styles with each of the methods.

*The Driver Engineer needs to constantly look into his box of tools to find the right approach to maximize the performance of his driver.*

Whether you need him to make a change in his technique or his belief system, become more integrated, or whatever, the intention is for you to determine what your driver needs, and then select a tool or strategy.

## The Learning Formula

The learning formula, MI + A = G (explained in Chapter 3), should be in the top drawer of your driver engineer's toolbox.

To help your driver make a change in technique, improve a physical skill, alter his state of mind, or build his confidence in his abilities, use the MI + A = G approach. Help him get a clear mental image of what he wants by asking him to imagine his goal in the specific area you are working on. Then, ask him to just be aware of what he is doing, or where he is in comparison to this goal. He doesn't have to try to achieve his goal. It will happen all by itself.

At one time, I felt that all a driver needed to do to make a change was to change his programming through the use of mental imagery. Even though that is still valid, there is a more efficient way—using the learning formula. On its own, MI or visualization can be just a fantasy or dream. When used in conjunction with A, it is a powerful, fast, and efficient method of learning or making a change. Jackie Stewart has said, "You can either have a vision or a dream. Dreams seldom come true, visions do come true." Vision is mental imagery plus awareness.

For example, if a driver needs to make a change in his technique, he can visualize doing that and he will make that change over a period of time. But a way of speeding up that change is by combining that mental image with awareness. Simply having the mental image will result in a slower change. Having the MI along with A will result in a much quicker change.

This formula may be the most valuable driver engineering tool in your toolbox. To use it, ask questions. Start with asking the driver to get a clear mental image of what he wants to achieve. Then ask him to rate on a scale of 1 to 5 or 10, how close he is to matching that mental image. He doesn't need to try to achieve what he is after; all he needs to do is become aware of how well he is doing. By putting a number on it, he has an objective rating of how far from his goal he is. In no time at all he will have achieved it.

## Awareness Building

One of the most important roles you, as the driver engineer, play is as an awareness builder for your driver. As I mentioned in Chapter 3, awareness is the key for your driver to operate at the unconscious competence with conscious awareness stage; as well as the most commonly absent variable in the learning formula, MI + A = G.

How do you raise your driver's awareness level? Just ask. In fact, asking questions is the core tool in engineering your driver. I said it before, and I'll say it again: your role is not to tell your driver *how* to drive. Your role is to get the maximum performance out of him. Asking appropriate and timely questions will help you do that.

In the past few years, coaching has become a popular approach to managing people in all sorts of activities, particularly in business. It seems that every manager in every business today is encouraged to coach their employees and co-workers. And the primary tool they suggest using is asking questions, with the primary goal of raising the person's awareness level. The same approach works with race drivers.

Let me start with an example, one different from the one I used in Chapter 3 to describe how I utilized the learning formula to help a driver use all the track on an oval.

Let's say your driver is too impatient during the opening laps of races, resulting in a number of crashes. You could tell him to be more patient, but how much good would that do? Not much, since you really haven't changed his mental programming whatsoever—and you are trying to get him to learn something from the outside in. You could, instead, ask him questions to lead him into using the learning formula:

• Do you think you have been too impatient in the past?

• On a scale of 1 to 10, where would you rate your patience level during the opening laps?

• On that same scale, what do you think would be ideal?

• What would that look and feel like to you, to have your patience level at that point on the scale?

The first two questions raise his awareness of where he is right now—the A. The second two questions help him develop the MI, the mental image of what he wants. Will asking these four questions just once completely change his patience level programming? Possibly but not likely. It is far more likely that you will need a few sessions of asking the same questions. After all, his programming did not come about from one isolated incident. It came about from a number of incidents, so it seems natural to expect it to take a number of question-asking sessions for a change to occur.

For you to be effective as a driver engineer, you can see that it is going to take some patience on your part. You may be thinking, "I don't have time to ask all these questions." Don't you? Do you have the time to tell him to be more patient, over and over again? Do you have the time to wait for repairs to be made to the car as a result of the crashes caused by his impatience, over and over again? I'm sure you get my point.

In my experience, while seeming to take a bit more time in the very beginning, asking questions will save you a significant amount of time in the long run. And, it is the only way of changing your driver's programming.

As I've said, your goal is not to tell your driver how to do something. It is likely that if you did attempt to tell him what to do, he would resist anyway. That is certainly one of the problems with telling him what or how to do something, but it is not the biggest problem.

No, the biggest problem is that if you tell him what or how to do something, it is unlikely that he will really learn it for himself. Sure, he may follow your instructions, but the second you are not there to tell him what to do again, he will go back to what he was doing before, back to his old programming. Again, learning from the inside out is far better than learning from the outside in.

Learning is programming. Learning something new requires changing old programming, or building new programming. Telling your driver what to do or how to do it rarely results in any changes to his programming.

If you want to keep busy and hear yourself talk, tell your driver what to do and how to do it. Then tell him again. And again. And again. . . .

If you want your driver to learn something, ask him questions that will lead to the changing of old programming, and the development of new programming—that will lead to learning. A driver engineer should act as a guide—a guide to further learning—rather than a conveyor of information—a teacher.

Asking questions is one of your most powerful tools. This may be even more important when you already know the answer yourself. Merely "telling" is rarely the best way to build someone's skills. Your driver will learn more if you ask him how well he performed a particular task than from being told, "Here's what you did wrong, and this is what you should do next time."

There are three important rules to keep in mind when asking your driver questions:

1. Keep your questions positive.
2. Keep your questions open-ended.
3. Keep your questions coming.

### SPEED SECRET #15
### Ask awareness-building questions—
### and then ask more.

Asking a question such as, "Why did you do that?" will not help much. It is not a positive question. Instead, try asking, "What did you do?"; "What would happen if you did this?"; "How could you accomplish that?"; and so on. These are positive questions, in that they lead to a solution, rather than simply focusing on the problem. A pretty good rule is do not use any question that begins with the word "why." It tends to infer blame. Doing any activity should not be taken personally. "Why" makes it personal. It also results most often in your driver becoming defensive, because it sounds too much like criticism. It rarely results in more awareness.

"What," "where," "when," and "how" are good words to start a question. Other words such as "notice," "observe," and "allow" are also good at involving your driver in the learning process. They lead your driver to find things out for himself—self-discovery.

Don't ask questions that will lead to a "yes" or "no" answer. Even if you think you know the answer, instead of asking, "Is the car under-steering in the slow corners?" ask "What is the car doing in the slow corners?" By asking an open-ended question, you will encourage more dialogue, and more awareness.

When I say keep your questions coming, I mean keep digging for the root of the problem, or the key to what you are after. Once you have solicited an answer to one question, dig one level deeper with your next question, and then another, and another. . . . Your objective is to get to the point where there are no other questions you could ask relating to the problem or subject.

Remember, as far as questions go, keep them positive, keep them open-ended, and keep them coming. With these rules in mind, asking questions will become the most-used engineering tool of them all.

### Sensory Input and Traction Sensing Sessions

Of all the tools in your driver engineering toolbox, sensory input and traction sensing is definitely one of, if not the, most effective. How does it work? You send your driver out onto the track for a session with the sole objective of taking in more sensory input.

The best way to gather more sensory input is to determine how much time you have to do this exercise, then split that up into four sessions. These sessions should be at least ten minutes in length, but not more than fifteen.

In the first session, ask your driver to focus on everything he can hear. Have him focus on the engine note, the sound coming from the tires, noise from the brakes, wind noise, and so on. Take in everything auditorily . . . whatever he can hear.

In the second session, have him focus on kinesthetic input—everything he can feel. He should notice all the vibrations through the steering wheel, pedals, and seat; the amount the car pitches, rolls, and squats; if the steering wheel gets lighter or heavier as the tires reach their limits; any vibration or chattering of the tires as they corner at the limit; and the g-forces working against his body.

In the third session, have your driver take in everything visually. He should focus on being more visually aware of everything. Ask him to focus on track surface irregularities and the horizon, notice any vibrations and movements of the steering wheel and other parts of the car, expand his view to take in more in his peripheral vision, and, if driving an open-wheel car, look for any changes in the surface of the front tires.

Finally, in the fourth session, have him go onto the track with the sole purpose of sensing the traction the tires have, feeling for the limit of adhesion, and noticing the car's feedback—the warning signs that the limit is approaching, or has gone past.

To make these sessions most effective, have your driver come into the pits after each one and debrief with you. Have him describe what he heard, what he felt, and what he took in visually. Try to prod him for as much info and feedback as possible by asking questions. If you do not have the time to debrief after each session, use some form of communications (radio or flags) to let him know when to change from auditory, to kinesthetic, to visual, and then to putting that together to sense traction. Have your driver sit and write down what he heard, felt, and saw at the end of the sessions.

### SPEED SECRET #16
### Use sensory input sessions on a regular basis to improve your driver's performance.

These four sessions are not a one-time deal. They should be done often, especially after switching to a new car or setup. The sessions should definitely be part of your driver's routine for learning a new track. The ultimate goal is to have your driver become more sensitive to all the sensory inputs. This will help him learn a new track quicker, become better at sensing when he is driving at the limit, and provide you with much more feedback for developing the car's setup.

Ultimately, there are three main benefits for sensory input and traction sensing sessions:

1. Quality input = quality output
2. Distracts conscious mind
3. Reduces driver errors

First, as I mentioned earlier, the better the quality and the greater the quantity of sensory information, the better the quality of the driver's performance. And, any time a driver focuses on one specific sensory input, the more sensitive he will become. It is much like a person who loses his sight. By focusing on and isolating the other senses, they become much more sensitive.

Second, the benefit of sensory input and traction sensing sessions is that they stop your driver from trying to drive fast—from thinking too much. Trying to go fast never works. Race cars are way too fast to drive at the conscious, trying level. They must be driven at the subconscious level, with the conscious mind observing, being aware.

Often, what your driver may need is a way to "distract" his conscious mind away from trying to drive fast. And what better distraction than having the conscious mind focused on providing the brain with more quality sensory input?

As an example, I was once coaching a driver on an oval track who was running lap times in practice that were about four-tenths of a second off where he had been the day before. Worse, this was after making a number of changes to the car to make it better. With the engineer on the radio telling him how many tenths off the quickest car he was, and the team owner telling him to carry more speed into turn 3, the driver was trying very hard to go fast. But he wasn't. Finally, as he came out of turn 2, I got on the radio and asked him to simply focus on what the car felt like for the next four laps. Within two laps he was back down to the times he had done the previous day, and was providing great feedback on the car that the engineer could really use to develop it.

I probably could have asked the driver to tell me what he ate last night, and it would have had much the same effect! No, it would not have provided his brain with more quality sensory input, but it would have gotten his conscious mind focused on something other than trying to drive fast. If you can learn to recognize when your driver is trying too hard—and all drivers do at some time—you can use this technique to great effect (though I do recommend asking your driver to focus on sensory input, not on what he ate last night!).

Third, sensory input and traction sensing sessions reduce the number and the extent of the driver's errors, both short-term and long-term. How?

Can you think of a driver who has a reputation for making "bad decisions" in the car? Often, the reason a driver makes poor decisions is because he lacks the information to base the decision on. It's like trying to make the decision to invest in a stock without having any past financial statements or annual reports.

If your driver dives down the inside of two other cars on the entry to a turn, with no hope in you-know-where of making it (and crashing), you and others may say he made a bad decision. You may wonder, "What was he thinking?"

If you really want to know why he crashed, you have to dig to the core of the problem. You may think the core is that he just makes poor decisions. But the reason, the cause, of the poor decision may be a lack of good information—a lack of quality sensory input.

In this example, what he saw as a large enough gap to make the pass, was not. He didn't have all the information—a complete picture. With more quality sensory input, your driver's decision making will improve—whether he currently makes good decisions or not.

Sensory input and traction sensing sessions can also minimize the effects of errors. Do you think experienced, champion race drivers make fewer errors than inexperienced drivers? I don't think so. The only difference is the experienced driver is better at minimizing the effects of them. I have definitely witnessed and experienced this myself.

When the experienced driver makes an error, such as turning into a corner too soon, he recognizes it immediately, makes a small subtle correction, and makes the best of the situation. When a less-experienced driver makes the same error, he may not recognize it until he is passing by the apex. At that point the correction is going to have to be much bigger, sometimes causing a further problem itself—or at least, having a drastic negative effect on the lap time.

So how does the experienced driver minimize the effects sooner? By recognizing the error sooner. How? By having more reference points. Most drivers have three reference points for each corner: turn-in, apex, and exit. Great race drivers, whether they are consciously aware of it or not, have dozens of reference points between those three. To become a great driver, your driver needs to practice sucking up more information about the track, so that he sees much more than just three reference points for each turn. He needs an almost continual path of reference points. And, these need to be in his mind at the subconscious level. That way, if he turns in too late for a corner, he recognizes this just a foot or so later—at the subconscious level—rather than when he is all the way to the apex. The sooner he recognizes it, the more subtle and effective the correction will be, and the less negative impact it will have. At that level, many drivers are not even aware that they made an error.

### SPEED SECRET #17
### Quantity and quality sensory input will lead to smaller errors.

As you already know, the better the quality and the more quantity of sensory information your driver puts into his brain, the better his performance will be. As I said earlier, this is similar to, but the opposite of the computer slogan, GIGO—garbage in, garbage out. In this case, it is quality in, quality out.

So when should you and your driver use the sensory input and traction sensing sessions? Often. When I've suggested to drivers to use these exercises, they sometimes claim that they do not have time. After all, they only have one practice session and then qualifying, and they certainly don't want to "waste" that time just taking in sensory input! That is exactly the time to be focusing on sensory input. The goal is to learn as quickly as possible, and this is one of the best ways of doing that.

### Speed Sensing

One of the most amazing things a race driver does is determine what speed the car needs to be traveling when entering a turn, and then slowing it to that exact speed. We all do this type of thing every time we come to a stop at a red traffic light. We look up ahead and make the decision to begin braking *now*, with *this* amount of pressure, and therefore we will stop at *that* point up ahead. No one tells us when to begin braking—there are no brake reference points on the street that I've seen.

This is even more difficult when we are not coming to a full stop—we're slowing to a specific speed, one that only your "gut feel" can tell you is at or near the limit of traction. The great drivers do that within a fraction of a mile per hour, consistently keeping the car at the very limit. This wouldn't be so difficult, or amazing, if the driver had the time to look at a speedometer while driving into the corners, but he doesn't.

If you used a radar gun to measure what speed a group of drivers entered one particular turn at, you might be surprised. As I said, the great drivers would consistently enter the turn at a speed that did not vary much more than a mile per hour. The not-so-greats' entry speed would vary by as much as five miles per hour or more!

Of course, I'm talking about slowing and setting the entry speed accurately and consistently so that the car is at or very near the limit. Almost anyone can consistently set the entry speed at something 10 or 20 miles per hour below the limit.

Until your driver can consistently set his entry speed within a mile per hour or two, he will never be able to begin shaving the last few tenths or hundredths of a second off his lap times. So his ability to sense speed is critical. Developing this without miles and miles of track time is not an easy thing to do. However, there are a couple of exercises to fine-tune his speed sensing abilities.

## Speed Sensing Exercises

The first exercise to improve speed sensing abilities is done in a street car on the street (if your driver is old enough). What you want him to do is practice estimating speed based on sensory input—not the speedometer. Start by cutting out a piece of cardboard that will cover the speedometer. As he drives, make note of the car's speed and then slip the cardboard cover in place. Have him change his speed a few times by accelerating and slowing down. Then ask him to put the car back to the original speed. Pull the cardboard cover off and check to see how accurate he is at sensing his speed. Do it again and again.

An alternative method is to leave the cardboard cover in place and pick a speed. Once he has reached what he feels is that speed, pull the cover off and check the numbers.

Encourage the driver to do these exercises by himself. If he does them over and over again, he will become more accurate and consistent at judging and establishing a specified speed. It doesn't matter that he is not working with the same kinds of speed he will be at on the racetrack. The main objective is that he can consistently set the speed of the car, within 1 mile per hour or so, using sensory input as his guide. That is accurate and consistent speed sensing.

The second exercise to improve a driver's speed sensing abilities requires a radar gun and is done on the track. Get yourself into a position with the radar gun where you can check your driver's speed just as he enters a corner. After a couple of laps to warm up, have him drive 10 laps with the goal of entering the turn at exactly the same speed. Of course, it does no good for him to drive slow during this exercise. He should be within a couple of tenths of his best lap times. With each lap, make note of the minimum speed he is traveling just as he turns in to the corner.

The goal, of course, is for him to consistently be at the same speed each lap as he enters the corner. If the corner entry speed varies more than 1 mile per hour, he needs to practice more. Ultimately, he should enter every corner at a consistent speed—within 1 mile per hour—for at least 10 laps in a row.

## Programming

Does telling your driver that he needs to make better decisions, turn in later, or concentrate longer help? Will it change anything? No, not unless you change his programming, for it is his programming that determines what decisions he makes, where he turns in, or how well he concentrates.

### Deprogramming, Reprogramming, and Programming

The first thing to understand is that it is more difficult to change a person's programming than it is to build his programming. If your driver has no prior programming for where to turn in for turn 1, for example, developing it is easier than changing any existing programming. Writing a brand-new piece of software, at least when it comes to drivers' minds, is easier than updating an old version.

This is why a driver with no experience at a particular track, or with a particular car, will sometimes be quicker than the old veteran. The veteran has to unlearn some things prior to learning the new things—he has a lot of preconceived notions. And again, simply telling him to change will not do anything. You have to change the programming.

Your job, if you are working with a veteran driver, is to help him deprogram and reprogram. If your driver is relatively inexperienced, your job is much easier. All you need to do is program him.

So how do you deprogram, reprogram, and program a driver? To begin to answer that question, let's go back to what I said earlier about how a driver develops his programming: either through physical programming, mental programming, and/or external/internal programming.

### Physical Programming

Albert Einstein once said, "A sure sign of insanity is doing the same thing over and over again and expecting something to change." How true! And yet, race drivers do that all the time. They go onto the track and drive it the same way over and over again, expecting to get better. Wait . . . I know just what you're thinking ("race drivers *are* insane!")— don't say it!

How many times has your driver gone onto the track simply to get "seat time," expecting to make some improvements. What is he doing? He's doing the same thing over and over again, expecting something to change. The problem is that most drivers do not have a plan, a strategy, specific objectives that result in a positive change.

Without a plan, strategy, or objectives for making a change to his programming, all he is doing is reinforcing the programming. He is physically programming doing the same thing as he has always done. And guess what? He will get even better at doing the same thing, even if that is not what he wanted to do.

One of your goals, whether your driver needs some reprogramming or not, should be to ensure that your driver never goes onto the track without having two or three specific objectives. Any more than three and his brain will most likely explode—it is somewhere between difficult and impossible to focus on more than three changes at one time while driving.

And when I say specific, I mean specific. An objective of going faster is not specific enough. Neither is braking later for turn 1, or accelerating earlier out of turn 2. The objectives must be well defined, such as braking at the 200 marker, braking 10 feet later, or beginning to accelerate 5 feet before the apex.

This is the only way of physically changing a driver's programming. Letting him go onto the track to "get seat time," "go faster," "figure out how to go faster," or "just go faster" means you are just as "insane" (in Einstein's words) as he is.

Also recall the learning formula: MI + A = G. The physical and mental go together, obviously.

### Mental Programming

Mental imagery (the MI of the learning formula), generally referred to as visualization, is mental programming.

Most race drivers will tell you that they use visualization. It is surprising just how many have heard about the technique of closing one's eyes and imagining driving a lap of the track while timing it with a stopwatch. Unfortunately, many of these drivers are not doing an effective job of programming.

There is a big difference between a driver closing his eyes and thinking about something—even imagining something—and real mental imagery or programming. The main difference is the level of relaxation of the driver's mind.

For mental imagery to be most effective, a driver must have his mind in a very relaxed, receptive state. To get to that state, a driver must learn to allow his mind to get to what is called the Alpha/Theta brainwave state (see *Speed Secrets 3: Inner Speed Secrets* for more details). Using an EEG (electroencephalogram), doctors and researchers can measure brainwave activity; they have defined four levels or states:

70

*A driver will only be able to do things on the track that he can see, feel, and hear in his mind before getting there. When your driver has specific things to work on in the next session, make sure he spends time getting that mental image clear in his mind. That's not just visualizing, it's using kinesthetic and auditory senses to make it more realistic.*

• Beta: The state you are in as you read this book. It is the conscious, awake, aware, alert, thinking state.

• Alpha: When you are relaxed, perhaps in that daydreaming or heading toward a meditative state, your brain is in an Alpha state.

• Theta: A very deeply relaxed state. You would most often experience this state just as you drift off to sleep, or in that hazy just-waking-up moment. Deep meditation is also at the Theta wave state.

• Delta: You are in a Delta state when you are sleeping.

At all times, a person is producing all four of the brainwave levels. For example, when you are fully awake and alert, your brain is producing mostly Beta waves, less Alpha, even less Theta, and very little Delta. While asleep, the opposite is true: mostly Delta, a little Theta, less Alpha, and very little Beta.

The Alpha/Theta state—when a person is producing primarily Alpha and Theta waves—is generally considered to be a super-learning state, as this is when the brain is most receptive, most easily programmed. Getting to that state requires getting into a relaxed position, breathing deeply and slowly, and being aware of the body as it lets go and relaxes. Once there, a driver can begin mentally imaging what he wants to deprogram, reprogram, or program.

One other key factor in effective mental imagery is using as many senses as possible. By definition of the word, *visualization* only uses one sense: visual. But the more senses you include, the more realistic it becomes to your mind, and the quicker and more effective the programming.

In Chapter 2 I asked you to close your eyes and imagine picking up, feeling, smelling, and tasting a lemon. Despite the fact that you had not gotten anywhere near an Alpha/Theta state, the imagery was pretty effective. The reason was the use of four senses. If you had imagined only seeing the lemon, your mouth may not have filled with saliva.

### SPEED SECRET #18
### Provide your driver with the opportunity to do
### mental programming.

So any time you ask your driver to use mental imagery, or even to imagine what something would be like, have him use at least the three senses used in driving a race car (visual, kinesthetic, and auditory). And any time your driver needs to make a change in his technique, or do something new, the best way to accomplish this is to start with your driver doing some mental imagery of the act.

### External/Internal Programming

What you say to your driver is just as important as what he says to himself. A great deal of his programming is a result of what other people say to him, and what he says to himself.

No matter how much belief a driver has in himself, if you tell him he makes too many mistakes too often, his programming will change. He will begin to believe that he makes too many mistakes. And do you know what happens when a driver believes he makes too many mistakes? His mind will do whatever it takes to match that belief, even if that means going out and making more mistakes.

It's sad but true that many drivers make bad decisions and crash cars primarily because of the programming their crew gives to them. Remember the story I mentioned in Chapter 2 of the crew chief who regularly reminded his driver "don't crash the car again," or "don't worry if you crash the car again, I can fix it." He thought he was doing the driver a favor, when really he was negatively programming him.

### Triggers

Imagine installing the latest, most powerful software package into your computer, but not having an icon on the desktop or start menu to access it. That is exactly what it would be like for your driver if he had the ideal program for driving, but not a "trigger." A trigger is an action and/or word that allows your driver to access, or activate, a mental program. Without it, your driver could have all the mental programming in the world, but will never activate it.

A trigger word or action works just like a gun's trigger. Once used, it fires the appropriate program.

Trigger words or actions should have some special meaning, or generate a vivid mental image, for your driver. As an example, to trigger a program to suck up sensory input, your driver may use the word "sponge" to see himself as a sponge, sucking up all there is to know. Other trigger words I've used either myself or with other drivers are "car dancing," "watch this," "party time," "play time," "time to kill," "crank it up," and "step it up." Trigger actions could include giving the steering wheel a quick squeeze, looking at a specific sign or message on the dash, or a hand signal from you. You may need to spend some time with your driver discovering just the right word, phrase, or action to use as a trigger word.

Then, when he is using mental imagery to program something, have him initiate it with a specific trigger word or action. That way, when he is in the heat of the battle, the second either of you says the trigger word or he uses the action, the program will kick in.

## Brain Integration

In Chapter 2 I talked about if your driver's brain is not integrated to the maximum level, it is unlikely that he will perform "in the zone." I also promised to give you a few exercises that will improve his level of integration. Of all the exercises that improve integration (if you want to know more, please read *Speed Secrets 3: Inner Speed Secrets*), Cross Crawl, Lazy 8s, and Centering are the most effective.

### Cross Crawl

As I mentioned earlier, the right hemisphere of your driver's brain controls the left side of his body, and vice versa. There is, or at least should be, cross lateral communication from one side of the body to the opposite side of the brain. This occurs at a high level when your driver is integrated; and not so much when he is less integrated (this is referred to as dis-integrated).

Almost any physical movement that connects one side of the body with the other will help your driver's level of integration. However, the simple cross crawl exercise may be the most effective. Here's how it works (try it yourself first).

While standing, raise your right leg, bending it at the knee, and bring your left arm over and touch the right knee. Return to standing. Then raise your left leg and touch the knee with your right hand.

*Doing Cross Crawls should be part of the ritual a driver does prior to every on-track session. It's an important key to triggering an "in the zone" performance behind the wheel.*

Return to standing, and then continue, alternating sides. You will find yourself marching in one place while alternately touching your knees with your opposite hand.

At first, do this at what is a comfortable rate for you, then slow it down to as slow a pace as you can. Doing it at a slow pace puts more stress on your sense of balance, improving it over time. Then speed it up until you are almost running on the spot while touching the opposite knee with your hands. At speed, this is a great exercise to get your driver's body warmed up prior to getting in the car.

There is a reason this exercise is called a cross crawl. When babies first begin to crawl, they most often do it in a unilateral motion. That is, they move their right hand and leg forward, then their left hand and leg, and so on—one side moves, and then the other. After a week or more for most babies, they change to a cross lateral crawling movement, where they move the right hand with the left leg, the left hand with the right leg, and so on. This cross crawling movement is the first step in the integration process of brain development.

Children who do not do enough cross crawling (often because they go almost directly from unilateral crawling to walking) may miss out on becoming fully integrated at an early age. In many cases, this leads to the child being slightly uncoordinated, or even having what some people call learning disabilities. By simply using the cross crawl exercise, many children have been able to "recover" from learning difficulties and have become far more physically coordinated. This exercise is extremely powerful.

Have your driver do cross crawls for about 30 seconds to two minutes each morning, in the evening, and especially just prior to getting into the race car. After doing this for a few weeks, he (and probably you) will begin to be aware of when he needs to become more integrated by doing more cross crawls. He will just feel better—more in the zone—when he is integrated.

My suggestion is that you do cross crawls with him prior to him getting in the car. Why? Two reasons. First, it will make him feel more comfortable—he will feel less self-conscious about doing this if someone else is doing it with him. And second, it will help your own personal performance. It is just as important for you to be integrated as it is for your driver.

## Lazy 8s

The second integration exercise is especially effective in helping integrate a person's vision. Just as there is a cross lateral connection between your driver's brain and body, there is a similar connection between his

*The Lazy 8 exercise is another critical element in a driver's pre-driving ritual. Most drivers will be amazed by how much more they observe and are aware of after doing this exercise.*

brain and eyes. In this case, the information coming into his right eye is sent primarily to the left hemisphere of his brain, and the information from his left eye is sent primarily to his right hemisphere. Once it is in his brain, the information is processed and constructed into what he "sees."

If that communication from his eyes to his brain, and from hemisphere to hemisphere is restricted in any way, your driver will miss a piece of the picture. At the speed he is traveling in the race car, missing just the tiniest piece of information may be catastrophic. And believe me when I say that a large percentage of drivers, even at the highest levels of professional racing, have visual processing problems resulting in incomplete visual pictures. Is it any wonder that many drivers make the wrong decision when trying to cut between a couple of cars in an overtaking maneuver; or that they make a small error (turning in too early for a corner, hitting a curb, etc.) that results in a slow lap time or a spin? Either of these may be the ultimate result of a visual processing problem that can be cured through the use of the lazy 8s exercise.

Have your driver stand with one arm stretched directly out in front of him, with a slight bend in his elbow and his hand in the thumbs up position. While he keeps his head steady, have him trace an imaginary figure eight lying on its side with his thumb, with his eyes following his thumb. Therefore, his eyes will be tracking this lazy 8 figure.

Have him do this exercise for about 20 to 30 seconds with each hand, and then with both hands. When doing it with both hands, don't have him interlock his fingers. Instead, just have him make two fists, place the knuckles from each hand together, and make a cross with his two thumbs. While flexing his arms and shoulders, have him trace the lazy 8 while focusing on the cross of his two thumbs. Again, make sure his head stays steady.

Watch his eyes closely while he does this. Do they move smoothly or are they notchy? Do they jump ahead in certain areas, skipping part of the figure eight? If so, they may be missing information in that area of his visual field. Do his eyes move congruently (together)? If you focus your vision on the bridge of his nose, you may notice that one of his eyes leads the other. That means that one eye is significantly less dominant than the other, which again means that he will probably be lacking some piece of visual information.

If you noticed some notchiness, jumping, or incongruity in his tracking, doing some lazy 8s for even 30 seconds to a minute will probably begin to make some improvement. And even if you didn't notice any problems with the way his eyes track, this exercise will benefit him. Again, it helps with brain integration, and specifically visual integration.

Your driver should do this exercise at least twice a day, and especially just prior to getting into the car. Many drivers report an immediate effect after doing this exercise. They say it helps them become more aware of what is going on around them, and much more perceptive. This, obviously, helps improve the quality of visual information being input into his brain.

Most people seem to think that good vision is something you are either born with or not, and that it is something that just goes away with age. And yet, they will agree that if a person does some form of physical exercise, their body will be and stay healthy for a longer period of time. Well, the same thing applies to vision. If you exercise it, it will improve and maintain its health and performance level longer.

### SPEED SECRET #19
### Ensure your driver does his pre-drive ritual, including cross crawls and lazy 8s.

## Centering

How important is it to the overall performance of the race car that it be well balanced? Critically important, right? But even if the car is perfectly balanced, if your driver's personal sense of balance is not near-perfect, can he drive the car to its limit? Or, if the car is not perfectly balanced, and neither is your driver, how effective is he going to be at reading exactly what the car needs?

The point is, of course, your driver's sense of balance is as critical as the car's, perhaps more so. Can it be improved? Yes. How? One way is by centering.

Centering is a technique used in martial arts. Have your driver lightly press the tip of his tongue to the roof of his mouth, toward the front behind his upper teeth, where peanut butter sticks. This area in a person's mouth is a strong acupressure point that triggers brain integration and an improved sense of balance. To make this fully effective, your driver should press a couple of fingers from one hand on a point just below his navel, and focus all his energy upon this center point of the body. In martial arts, this point is called the "chi."

Obviously, your driver cannot drive the car while pressing his navel. But he can place the tip of his tongue on the roof of his mouth, particularly in high stress areas of the track. For example, as he approaches the fastest turns on the track, or when trying to brake very late for a corner, he centers (placing his tongue on the roof of his mouth) and breathes. This way, when he most needs to be integrated, sensitive to what the car is telling him, and balanced, he is.

This centering technique also has a stress-relieving, or relaxing effect. An uptight, stressed-out driver will rarely perform at his peak. By centering, your driver will be more relaxed, learn at a quicker rate, and perform at his best more consistently. Of course, this applies to you as well. In fact, the more centered you are, the more centered everyone around you will be, including your driver; not to mention your own performance level being better.

If your driver practices centering on a regular basis, you and he will notice a difference in and out of the car. Just before he leaves pit lane to go onto the track, either signal or tell your driver to "center." Over a short period of time, this will trigger a calm, focused, integrated race driver—just what you wanted.

## Enhancing Track Memory

Is your driver one of those who can learn a racetrack in half a dozen laps or so? If so, great. If not, is there anything you can do to help him learn quicker? Yes. In fact, many of the driver engineering techniques you are already using will do that. But there is one specific exercise your driver can use to improve his ability to learn and memorize a track quicker.

This exercise occurred to me as I was reading Bill Russell's book, *Russell Rules*. The basketball great wrote of how, as a kid, he would look at books of paintings by Leonardo da Vinci and Michelangelo, then close the books and re-draw them from memory. He was exercising his visual memory—his ability to memorize how things look. Through practice, he improved his ability to visually take in information, place it in his memory data bank, and access it later. This helped later when he would visualize his moves on the court, or those of the players he was defending.

I realized, as I was reading this, that I did a similar thing when I was young. I spent hours and hours drawing imaginary and real racetracks and the line a car would drive to be quick. I also drew cars, both ones that I imagined and ones I copied from photos. I became good at this; I'm sure that is one of the reasons it doesn't take me long to memorize a track. Your driver can do the same type of thing—now.

Have your driver practice viewing a picture, and then try to re-create it later. By doing this, his visual memory will improve. He does not have to be a good artist to do this exercise. The objective is not to see how well he can draw. It is to improve his ability to observe the details of something, to memorize those details, and to recall them when needed.

Of course, he could and should do this exercise with his auditory and kinesthetic senses as well. Listening to a piece of music, for example, then shutting it off and trying to re-create it will have the same effect for his auditory sense. And perhaps your driver should take up sculpting to fine-tune his sense of feel; or he could practice imitating the physical movements of any athlete (a basketball or tennis player, a skier, or a skateboarder, for example).

The goal is to see, hear, or sense something kinesthetically, and then re-create that from the mental image in his head. The more he does this exercise, the better he will get at memorizing a track.

The sooner a driver has a perfect mental image in his memory of every minute detail of the racetrack, the quicker he will be. This is particularly important on tracks that have "blind" corners, where the driver cannot see the track ahead until he is practically there. Having great track memory is critical to being consistently fast. Of course, being a great "sponge," with the ability to soak up sensory input will help as well.

## Withholding Lap Times

The one thing that most often leads to a driver trying too hard to go fast is when he pays too much attention to his lap times. If your driver has a goal of a certain lap time in his head, he will try everything he can to reach that, even if that means driving at the conscious level.

There is a time and place for lap times. For many drivers, that time is not during a qualifying session. Sometimes it is more productive to not let your driver know what lap times he is turning when qualifying. With many of today's cars having the lap times displayed on the dash, you may have to either reprogram the dash so it is not shown, or simply cover it with a piece of tape.

If you think about it, or more importantly if your driver thinks about it, knowing the lap times is not important. After all, the goal is to continually work at being faster, no matter what lap time he just turned. If he turns a lap time even a second or two quicker than he ran in practice, why not go for more? And, at any time, you can make the decision to call him into the pits if you think the time he has turned is fast enough, and you do not want him to risk the car any more.

The other reason for not allowing your driver to know what lap times he is running is that he will rarely exceed his expectations. Many, if not most, drivers go out for qualifying with a lap time in their head, whether they are aware of it or not. Usually, this lap time is based on what they have done in the past or in practice, what the competition has been doing, and what others think will be the pole time. The problem is the track can change. I've seen it way too often that a driver goes out for qualifying with a specific lap time in his head, a 1:12.5 for example, and reaches that within the first couple of laps. The problem is that the track conditions changed, for the better, meaning that to stay in the qualifying position that he expected, he would need to do a 1:12.0.

## Control your driver's focus—keep it on his performance.

The key point here is, a driver will rarely exceed his expectations. If he has no expectations, or no way of knowing when he has reached them, it is easier for him to continue to push for more. A driver should never put a limit on his performance. Lap times often do that.

### Replaying Past Successes

In Chapter 2, I suggested that most drivers do not have any defined process for triggering an ideal state of mind that helps produce a great performance. So how do you help induce your driver's performance state of mind? The best technique I know of is to simply ask your driver to recall, and replay in his mind, a great past performance. The interesting thing is that this great performance does not have to be while racing. It could be anything, from playing another sport to a positive business experience, or while participating in a hobby or a great personal relationship experience.

Anything that, when told to you by your driver, results in him being extremely positive, happy, energized, and calm will do the trick. I use this technique often when engineering drivers, particularly just prior to a qualifying session. I like to find out beforehand about a great performance in the driver's past, and then ask him to tell me about it just before qualifying. I've had drivers relate stories about a past hockey or soccer game, a previous qualifying session or race, or a positive business experience. In each case, I could see it on their faces that they were in a positive, performance state of mind after telling me their story.

Another technique that I like to use with drivers is to have them walk to their cars like they imagine Michael Schumacher would. In other words, act like Schumacher. I'm sure you have noticed this yourself, how some drivers just look like they are there to win, and others do not.

Most of that is in the way they present themselves—the way they walk.

If your driver models his walk after Schumacher, for example, his state of mind cannot help but be closer to ideal. Used in conjunction with relating a past experience, it is an extremely effective tool.

## Building Confidence

A driver's confidence level is a part of his belief system. If he believes in his own abilities, the car's abilities, the team's, and your abilities, he is far more likely to perform at his maximum level.

Where does a driver's confidence level come from? A big part of it comes from you and the team around him. If you or the team have any doubt whatsoever in his abilities, he will pick up on it, and it will affect his confidence—and performance. It is very difficult for anyone to totally believe in himself if other people around him do not.

Can you fool him into believing that you have confidence in him when you don't? No. However, if you have no expectations of results for your driver, just a belief that he can perform at his own maximum level (which everyone in this world can), then he will feel your confidence in him.

If the energy level of the team is low, your driver will also be more likely to doubt his abilities. I believe it is primarily up to the driver to build the team's enthusiasm, energy, and confidence level—to inspire the team—but there are times when you may need to do that on his behalf. At those times, it is best if it appears to be coming from the driver. The most successful race teams have always had a strong driver who inspired the team, with people surrounding him who may have been doing just as much, but had the confidence and ego-control to let the driver take the credit.

Building confidence often comes down to external programming. No matter how confident a driver is, if you or anyone else on the team lets on that he is not believed in, his confidence and therefore performance will suffer. It is up to you to ensure that the team does all it can to externally program your driver's belief system, building his self-confidence. That is why you must always show trust in his abilities to read the car, to the point of sometimes going against what the data acquisition and your gut feeling tells you. If you go with what your driver wants, yes it may sometimes be the wrong direction. But the confidence built by you trusting his judgment will pay huge dividends in the long term, sometimes even overpowering what is truly right for the car!

## Building Intensity

It may seem hard to believe, but some drivers are too relaxed when they get behind the wheel of the race car. It is not that they need to be more excited, it is just that their energy or intensity level is too low for the situation. Other drivers, of course, need to be calmed down. It is important for you to read your driver's energy, or intensity, level.

You may need to get your driver to physically yell in his helmet as he is leaving pit lane, or do some form of physical activity prior to getting into the car (some fast cross crawls, riding a bike, running on the spot, etc.).

It really is amazing that athletes in every other sport do some form of physical warm-up prior to performing, and yet most race drivers do little or nothing. Having your driver do some physical warm-up prior to driving may give him a big edge over his competition.

## Observation

One of the most obvious, but often overlooked tools in your driver engineering toolbox is actually standing in various areas around the racetrack, observing your driver perform. Once again, it does not matter how much experience you have driving a race car, for you are not there to tell him what to do. Your only job is to observe and report what you noticed. By doing that, you raise his awareness. In fact, I know of people who had never been to a race in their lives who have helped drivers learn something, simply by asking a few questions. In fact, the lack of knowledge led to naïve questions that an experienced person most likely would have overlooked.

All you really need to do is compare your driver and car to others. If you notice, for example, that your driver seems to be braking earlier than other drivers, turning into the corner later, or is more abrupt on the throttle (all things that practically anyone can and will notice when standing near the edge of the track), you shouldn't tell him that he

*Practically anyone can help your driver raise his awareness simply by observing him and the car on the track. Comparing him to other drivers/cars is the key, and then asking questions to make him aware of what he's doing and what he could do better.*

needs to change what he is doing. Instead, all you need to do is ask him what he is doing, where, and how. That will increase his awareness of what he is doing, and he will most likely fix whatever needs to be fixed on his own.

If you tell him that you noticed he brakes earlier than other drivers he may get defensive, giving excuses as to why he is doing that. Instead, ask, "Where do you brake? Is it possible to brake later? What would happen if you did?" By asking these questions, you are not threatening or questioning his abilities, you are helping him become more aware of what he is doing, you are getting him to think about what he is doing, you are improving his awareness level. With that in hand, he will be able to make the necessary improvements in his driving.

If your job is to engineer the race car, you may be thinking that you have to be in pit lane while your driver is on the track. Sure, there are times when it is more efficient to be in pit lane, but most of the time you will accomplish more by going out and observing your driver and car on the track. You will definitely learn more about the car's handling watching it in a corner than you will by seeing it zoom by the pits.

As Carroll Smith said, "Another thing that amazes me is how few of my peers I see out on the track watching the cars. I can do no good for anyone in the pits—and neither can you. Get out there on the corners where you can see your car, your driver, and all the rest. You will be amazed at what you can discover."

## SPEED SECRET #21
### Build both your and your driver's awareness by observing.

Again, I want to make this very clear: Do not use observation as an excuse to begin telling your driver what to do. You are not there to instruct him. You are there to observe, be an extra set of eyes, and raise his awareness by reporting what you saw (without any judgment) and asking a few questions. Unless your driver considers you to be a better race driver than he is (which most successful drivers do not feel about anyone else), the second you begin taking what you observed and using that to tell him how to drive, you will ruin any chance of helping him improve.

*Have your driver make notes on a track map after each session. It helps develop his awareness, advances the process of programming track references, and improves his ability to provide feedback to the team.*

## Debriefing

No matter what level or type of racing you and your driver are involved in, after every session the two of you must have a debriefing. This may only take a minute or two, or it could last for hours. Your main goal is to determine what the objectives should be for the next session, to make further improvements.

One of the first things you should do in a debriefing session is to hand your driver a track map and have him debrief with it. Ask him to make notes on the track map, writing down what gear he is in, and what the car is doing in the braking zone and at the entry, middle, and exit phase of each corner. Then, have him rate his driving on a scale of 1 to 10 in each section of the track, with a 10 representing the car being driven at the very limit and 1 being well away from the limit.

The exact number he puts on "how close to the limit was I" for each section of the track is not important. Every driver will perceive the limit as something a little different, so it is not something that you could even compare from one driver to another. The goal is simply to help your driver become fully aware of whether he is driving every section of the track at the limit.

The interesting thing is that most drivers will have to recalibrate their ratings as they improve. Often, a driver will believe he is driving at a 9 or 10 on the "limit" scale for a little while. Then, with a bit more experience, and a better sense or feel for the traction limit, he will perceive that same cornering speed as only a 6 or 7. With time, what was once a 10 will only be a 7. Again, the number is not important. There is no point in even discussing or trying to suggest to him that it should be something other than what he felt and reported. It is only an exercise to improve his awareness.

It is important to go through this process prior to him learning what his lap times are compared to others. Once a driver begins to think in terms of how he compared to the competition, the accuracy of his awareness and feedback will suffer.

As he goes through this process, he will become more aware of things the car is doing than if you simply asked him. For most people, the act of writing it down leads to a fuller awareness level. Without that awareness, you will not have the information you require to make the car better, nor will your driver have the awareness of what he needs to change to improve his driving.

Through the exercise of putting a number on how close to the limit he is driving the car in each area of the track, he will become completely aware of where there is room for improvement.

## Establishing Strategies and Objectives

A car engineer would never be successful at developing the car without some type of plan. The same thing applies to developing your driver. Without a plan, one of two things will happen. Either no change—and no improvement—will take place, or the wrong changes will take place. That is why establishing objectives prior to every on-track session is critical, even if the objective is to not make any change so that your driver can make note of some subtle change to the car.

It is a complete waste of time, and a disservice to your driver, if you let him head onto the track without two or three specific objectives. These objectives may relate just to the car, in terms of feedback on a particular setup change, or they may all have to do with a change in driving technique. The point is, without making a change, it is doubtful at best that the car or your driver will improve.

**SPEED SECRET #22**
**Ensure your driver has no more than three very specific objectives each time he heads onto the track.**

One of the best ways of doing this is by telling him what questions you plan to ask after the session. If, for example, you tell him you are going to ask him where he begins braking for turn 1, what he does with the steering wheel just after turn-in for turn 4, and whether the car understeers or oversteers at the exit of turn 8, you have helped him establish three specific objectives for the session. You have helped focus him.

## Driver Notes

How effective is a car engineer who does not keep any notes of the changes he makes to the car? Not very, right? The same thing applies to the driver. One of the key objectives of driver engineering is to ensure the driver never makes the same mistake twice, or has to learn the same thing twice.

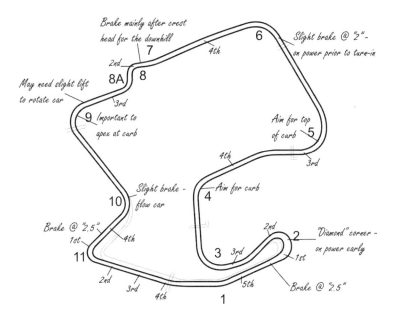

*One of the most important tools for raising the driver's awareness—and to improve his feedback on the car—is to have him make notes on a track map. These notes should include every little detail about what he sees, feels, and hears (lots of references), how the car is handling, and what he is doing to the car.*

Therefore, you should encourage your driver to keep extensive notes in a journal of some type. I recommend that at each track you go to, he draws his own track map. Why is that better than just using a printed track map that the track or the data acquisition system supplies? Because it is important for your driver to draw the track as he sees it, not necessarily as it really is. To back up his drawn map, he may also want to keep a copy of a printed track for extra reference and comparison.

On this map he should make notes that relate to how he drives it, such as the gears used in each turn, specific reference points ("turn-in at the crack in pavement," "apex at the end of the curbing," etc.), elevation and surface changes, and good places to pass. He should make note of any particularly challenging pieces of track, and why. He will also want to record the date, the car, his best lap time, the fastest car's lap time, and weather conditions. This information becomes invaluable the next time he races at this track, whether he is driving the same car or not.

Your driver should make notes of all the things he has learned each day at the track. If that isn't a pretty extensive list, either you or he are not doing your jobs. I don't care how much experience a driver has, he will always be learning something new—if he and you are aware. Obviously, writing down what he has learned will reduce the chances of him forgetting and having to learn the lesson all over again (at great expense, in most cases).

Finally, he should rate his own performance on a scale of 1 to 10 for each session on a race weekend (or the day for a test day), and make note of how he felt and what he did leading up to it. That way, over a period of time, a pattern will begin to emerge—one that spells out a routine that will lead to consistently great performances. For example, if he notices that whenever he does some type of physical warm-up prior to driving, or that a certain phrase used by you or another team member seems to lead to "9" performances, you and he know what to do in the future.

## SPEED SECRET #23
### *Your driver should keep notes on every aspect of his driving.*

If he makes note of his state of mind, his level of energy and intensity, what he has eaten over the past day or two, who has been around him and what they have said, how confident or nervous he felt, it becomes much easier to develop a pre-race ritual that will lead to a great performance. Without writing it down, it is easy to miss the pattern.

# Chapter 5

# When to Engineer the Driver

Knowing when to engineer your driver, and when not to, is as important as knowing how.

Throughout this book I assume your driver has some level of competency and experience. If your driver is just starting, then coaching or engineering may not be appropriate—teaching and instructing may be. If your driver is at the very beginning of his driving career, then being taught and instructed at one or more of the professional race driver training programs or schools will be most effective. But once past that stage, coaching and driver engineering is the best approach.

One of the things that makes a true driver engineer is the ability to recognize when a driver needs teaching or instructing. If the engineer is not experienced or knowledgeable enough to provide that teaching/instructing, then he should look elsewhere to provide it. A great driver engineer is not working with the driver for the ego trip. He is not doing it to say he has made all the difference in the world to the driver. A driver engineer will also know when and how to help motivate a driver.

## Skill-Will Matrix

There are times, even for an experienced driver, when he requires some teaching. This is typically when he has little to no knowledge or experience with a technique. And even though it is rare that you would have to worry about motivating a race driver (most would not be racing if they needed a lot of motivating), there are times when it is necessary.

So there are times as a driver engineer where you need to teach your driver, times you need to help his motivation, and times you need to coach him. How do you know when to do what? Try placing your driver in the Skill-Will Matrix.

|  | LOW SKILL | HIGH SKILL |
|---|---|---|
| **HIGH WILL** | Teach | Coach |
| **LOW WILL** | Motivate and teach | Motivate |

When you consider this matrix, you begin to see just how complex and challenging a role you have.

But let's get one thing straight right now. *You* cannot directly motivate a driver. Only he can motivate himself. Yes, you can give him the tools, the information, the incentives, and whatever else helps him to become motivated, but only the driver can motivate himself.

Once again, the best tool for helping your driver motivate himself is to ask questions. For example, you might ask the following:

• What is it that you enjoy most about racing?
• What is the best part about being a race driver?
• What is the most rewarding part of racing?
• What do you enjoy about racing?
• What don't you enjoy about racing?
• On a scale of 1 to 10, where would you rate your level of motivation?

I'm sure you recognize the pattern. The first three questions are there to build his MI, and the last three his A. Together, his MI and A will result in the goal—a motivated driver. If not, then your driver had best look to another sport or profession. For without motivation, your driver will rarely perform at his peak.

### Asking for Permission

Do you want to know the surest way of alienating your driver? Coach or engineer him when he doesn't want it. Turn the tables for a moment.

No matter how much you need the help yourself, are you always willing to accept it? I doubt it. No one wants it all the time.

Prior to coaching or engineering your driver, ask permission to do so. Without his permission, you will never be successful.

Funny how that works, isn't it? You need to ask for permission to ask questions. Sounds like a lot of asking, doesn't it? You bet it is. But it's the only way.

If your driver comes off the track in a poor state of mind because another driver did something he didn't appreciate, because the car had not performed well, or because he had made a few too many errors, it may not be the ideal time to engineer him. A good driver engineer knows when to keep his mouth shut.

### SPEED SECRET #24
### Know when to teach, when to coach, when to motivate, and when to engineer your driver.

Perhaps that is the time for his regular post-session debriefing, and then when that is complete, ask him if it would be okay if you asked him some questions. If he is not in the mood, don't push it. If he is not ready for it, all the driver engineering tricks in the world will not be effective.

## Managing Resistance to Driver Engineering

The most difficult driver to engineer is the successful one. Why? Because he doesn't need any help—at least that is what he thinks. The frustrating thing is that drivers who have early success in their careers often do not live up to expectations for this very reason. They think that since they are successful "right out of the box," they do not have to work at improving.

The drivers who are most successful, who go on to true greatness, are always open and willing to learn more and improve.

Breaking through the barrier, getting your driver to not only accept, but actively search out and embrace any opportunity to learn and improve, can be a challenge.

## Relieving Stress and Emotions

Think back to times in your life when you were stressed out over a heavy work load, or when you had become too emotionally involved in something. How much did you learn during this time? How effective were you? How was your own personal performance?

There is no doubt that your driver will not perform well, or learn much, when his stress level is high or he is overly emotional about something. Therefore, your job at times will be to recognize when one of these distractions is a factor, and to help your driver manage it.

I wish there was one specific tool or technique that you could use to recognize when your driver is stressed or emotionally charged, and to relieve that stress and neutralize his emotions. Unfortunately, there is not one simple trick. The key is being aware of these factors, and being sensitive to them. By doing that, over a period of time, you will learn to read and manage your driver's stress level and emotions.

# Chapter 6

# Driving Technique

I have no intentions of giving you all you need to know about the physical technique of driving a race car. You can, and should, develop some understanding of these techniques, but this is not the place. As I mentioned earlier, I recommend that you attend a race driver training program or school to acquire some basic knowledge. I also recommend reading *Speed Secrets* and *Speed Secrets 2*—practically everything you will ever need to know to engineer your driver from a driving technique point of view is covered in them.

Having said that, I would like to cover a few specific areas of driving technique that you may use someday with your driver. Some of these apply strictly to road racing, others relate to road racing and oval tracks.

I need to repeat what I said earlier. Your role is not to teach your driver how to drive the race car. Your role may be, though, to suggest some strategies that will help his driving technique. That is why I'm presenting the following technique-related items. My hope is that by giving you some examples of situations your driver may be facing, you will be better prepared to engineer him through the problem. Although these examples are but a few of the hundreds, or thousands, potentially facing you and your driver, by presenting them here, you will be more likely to recognize them. You will also be better prepared to deal with others not presented here.

## The Limit

When one driver can make a car go faster than another in the same car, is that because one driver is not driving the car to its limit? Not necessarily. It may be that the slower driver has created an artificially low limit.

For example, some drivers are better at keeping the car balanced during corner entry than others. That superior balance leads to a higher limit. You could argue that the slower driver was not driving the car at its ultimate limit, and you would be correct. However, if he is driving the car at its limit of traction—even though it is lower since he has not entered the corner with the car as well balanced—he really is at the limit.

The point I want to make is that you must recognize when your driver is not driving at the limit, and when he has created an artificially low limit. There is no point in trying to engineer him into driving faster when he is already driving at the limit. No, in this case you must engineer him into keeping the car better balanced. If you can do that, he will automatically drive the car faster—he already knows where the limit is since that is where he has been driving the car all along.

So how do you go about engineering your driver into keeping the car better balanced? I admit that this will be a difficult challenge for you, as 90 percent of the time it comes down to how well, and when, your driver trails off the brakes and makes the transition back to the throttle. The timing must be right, and it must be done perfectly smooth—seamlessly. And of course, what is right for one corner will often not be right for the next corner. Your driver may require some professional coaching in this area.

Identifying how well he finishes his braking and transitions to the throttle is the challenge. Sometimes, with a trained eye, you can observe it from the side of the track. Other times you can see it from the data acquisition traces. And other times still, it comes from what your driver says as you debrief and ask awareness-building questions. In fact, in many cases, if you just ask the right question, your driver will become aware of it and fix the problem on his own.

Depending on the experience and competency level of your driver, perhaps the biggest challenge he faces is being able to consistently drive the race car at its limit. Through the years, the one question race drivers have asked me more than any other is, "How do I know when I'm at the limit?" That, and knowing how to get to the limit is what driving a race car fast is all about. Helping your driver reach that limit is also one of the biggest challenges facing the driver engineer.

*Driving a car at the limit is one of the most challenging things anyone can strive to do. Perhaps the only thing harder is explaining to a driver how to do it. Fortunately, a driver engineer does not have to do that—he just has to help the driver figure it out for himself. That's all!* Kent Regan

The first question, "How do I know when I'm at the limit?" may be the easiest part of this problem to handle. In fact, the question almost answers itself after a driver spends some time doing sensory input and traction sensing sessions. The reason many drivers do not know their limit is because they have never focused on sensing the limit. Given a little time to practice sensing it, they will develop a fine sensitivity to it.

The question of how to reach the limit may be more difficult. Some drivers find the limit by going way over it, and then—after repairing the crash damage—dialing it back a little. Other drivers continually inch up on the limit, taking little pieces of extra speed until they finally reach it. Although this is the safest way of reaching the limit, it can take more time than is available. By the time the driver is close to the limit, the race event is over!

The ideal approach is to make big enough jumps in speed to get to the limit quickly, but not so big that your driver goes too far over the top. Again, having a finely tuned sense of traction is the first requirement. That comes from focused practice—sensory input and traction sensing sessions. The second requirement is the right mindset, the right approach. That approach is summed up by the first sentence in this paragraph: *make big enough jumps in speed to get to the limit quickly, but not so big that your driver goes too far over the top.*

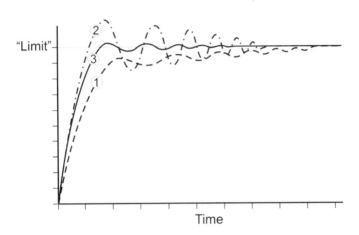

*Three approaches to driving the limit: No. 1 creeps up on it slowly, taking small steps; No. 2 takes big steps, often going way beyond; and No. 3 takes medium steps, going slightly beyond the limit and bringing it back—homing in on the limit.*

And speaking of going beyond the limit, some people believe the only way to truly know it is to go past it. In other words, until the driver has spun the car, he will never know the limit. The unfortunate thing is that many drivers spin the car but never learn much from it. That's where you, the driver engineer, come in.

It is very important—critical, in fact—to take some time after a spin and evaluate why it happened, and what can be learned from it. Often, it was not an increase in speed that caused the spin, it was an error in technique that went along with the faster speed. Of course, the obvious conclusion after carrying more speed through a turn and spinning is to blame the extra speed. That is why your driver, and you, need to take a good look at a spin to determine the real cause. More times than not, when a driver carries a bit more speed into a turn, the anxiety that accompanies it impairs his technique, which is what really causes the spin.

## Corner Priorities

If you were to ask a race driver which is the most important corner on a road racing circuit, you would most likely get the response, "the corner leading onto the longest straightaway." That has been the standard approach to driving race cars for many years, at least since Alan Johnson's book, *Driving in Competition*, was released in 1971. The theory goes that the corner leading onto the longest straight is most important, the one leading onto the next longest is second most important, and so on until there are no more corners leading onto straightaways. Then, the corners at the end of straightaways are next most important and, finally, corners connecting corners are the least important.

Although this advice had been around for a long time, and been used by lots of drivers to great success, I updated the approach in my *Speed Secrets* book a few years ago. The new theory is that the most important corner is the fastest one that leads onto the longest straight, then the next fastest one leading onto a straight, and so on down to the slowest corner leading onto a straight. Then, it is the fastest corners at the end of straights and, finally, the corners connecting other corners.

The difference is that the place you are going to gain and lose the most amount of time is in the fast corners. There are at least two reasons for this:

If you make an error in a first or second gear corner leading onto a straightaway, it will not hurt you as much as if you make an error in a third, fourth, or fifth gear corner leading onto a straightaway. This is true even if the straightaway after the fastest corner is not as long as the one following the slower corner. Take a look at Road Atlanta for example. Turn 7, which leads onto the long back straight, is a first or second gear corner. If you make a small error and lose 2 miles per hour, it will not hurt your overall lap time as much as if you made an error and lost 2 mph in the very quick turns 12 or 1. In other words, it is more difficult to make up a loss of 2 mph at 120 mph, than it is at 50 mph.

Fast corners are more difficult. If they are more difficult for your driver, they are more difficult for other drivers as well. So if your driver can get them right, he will gain an advantage over his competition.

### SPEED SECRET #25
### Prioritize your driver's focus on the
### most important corners.

This not only applies to how your driver approaches learning and perfecting a track, but also to how you approach developing the car. If a compromise must be made between having the car work best in one of two turns, as it often does, always chose making it handle best in the fastest corner.

So when your driver begins fine-tuning his line and technique around a racetrack, help him prioritize his work load. I said it earlier: a driver cannot go onto the racetrack and work on perfecting everything and every corner at one time. He needs to pick two or three of the most important pieces, and work on them first. Then he can move on to the next. That is why it is critical to understand which corners are most important in terms of lap time. Do not let your driver fuss and fret over perfecting the least important corner on the track until he has truly perfected the rest. Set out a priority list of corners, and have him work on his driving with that perspective. You can use the same list in developing the car.

### The Line and Car Control

Let me ask a couple of questions. First, just how important is the ideal cornering line to a driver's overall speed? How important are a driver's car control skills—his ability to drive the car at the very limit? Which is most important, the cornering line or your driver's car control skills?

Yes, you could answer with "both," and be correct. But that's too easy an answer. I believe that a driver who drives perfectly on the ideal line, but below the traction limit will not be as fast as a driver who drives off-line, but at the limit. In other words, if you had to choose, the ability to drive the car at the limit is more important than being on the ideal line. The reason I believe this is because I've tested and proven it.

Of course, I'm talking about being reasonably close with either. If a driver is on the wrong side of the track, all the car control skills in the world will not make him faster than someone driving the ideal line; and, a driver 20 miles per hour off the limit will not win even if he is driving the perfect line.

Now, this is not an excuse for your driver to not drive on the ideal line. But what I'm saying is if he has to slow the car down to get it to follow the ideal line, he would be better off giving it up. I've seen too many drivers fight the car so much to get it to follow the perfect line—forcing it to hit the right apex, for example—that they scrub off more speed than is gained by driving that line. Sometimes it is better for the driver to let the car go where it wants, where it needs to go to maintain momentum. And if the car won't go where he wants, maybe it is time to look at tuning its handling.

With this in mind, I want to make one thing clear: the line is very important. In fact, one of the biggest challenges a race driver faces is determining which line to use. Many times a driver has the option of driving a corner in one of two ways:

1. Brake hard, slowing the car down, turn in late toward a late apex, and then stand on the throttle; or

2. Brake a little lighter, carrying more speed through the corner, which may mean getting back on the throttle a little later.

Which option he chooses is dependent upon the type of car (how much engine power it has, its cornering and braking ability, tires, etc.), the corner's radius (and therefore relative speed), and the amount of traction the track provides (banking, bumps, surface, etc.).

## SPEED SECRET #26
### Drive the car at the limit, and the line will take care of itself.

Computer simulation programs can map out the exact line that will result in the very quickest lap time. Of course, these programs are well beyond the financial means of all but the top Formula One teams. You can also argue that when computers begin telling the driver what line to drive, maybe it's time to rethink the whole sport. Until that time, the drivers themselves will determine the perfect line. How do they do that? Primarily through traction and speed sensing, backed up by what the stopwatch and/or data acquisition system indicates.

Which again is another reason why your driver's traction and speed sensing abilities are so critical. Often, a driver will choose one particular line and method of driving a corner, believing it is the fastest way, only to have the data acquisition (and the competition) prove it is not. The reason the driver chooses that line and method is not because he is unaware of what he is trying to achieve (the fastest lap). It is because he is not sensitive enough to the car's traction and speed.

Therefore, to help your driver make the best decisions as to which is the best line and style for each and every corner, work with him to develop the sensitivity of his traction and speed sensing abilities. Do that, and he will make the right decisions at the innate, automatic— subconscious—level.

### Driving Style

It seems only appropriate at this point to talk about driving style in a little more detail. Each race driver has his own unique style of driving the race car. Some drivers brake relatively early and lightly for corners, carry lots of speed in, maintaining speed all through the turn, and smoothly squeeze back on the throttle. Others brake as late as possible, standing the car on its nose, rotate the car quickly at turn-in, and then stand on the gas again. It's the smooth, flowing style versus the point-and-shoot style.

Of course, those are only two of the thousands of different styles. Driving style is also determined by how much or how little a driver likes to trail brake into the turns, how quickly or slowly he initiates the turn-in with the steering wheel, how smooth or abrupt he is with the brake and throttle application, and so much more.

Some race car engineers I've talked to claim that there is only one driving style that is optimum—that will ultimately lead to the quickest lap. The reasoning is that the laws of physics dictate that there is one ideal way to drive a race car. I certainly do not disagree—in theory.

However, the ideal style for one car in one corner may not be the ideal style for another corner on the same track. Therefore, the ideal style may be a combination of many styles—a point-and-shoot style in one or two corners, a smooth flowing style in a couple of others, and some varying compromise between the two in others still.

Certainly, altering driving style to suit specific corners is something that all good race drivers do to some varying extent. But having your driver change completely from one style to another, from one corner to the next, may be just too much to ask from any human being. That is why some drivers will always have different driving styles, some suiting certain cars and tracks more than others. Until computers start driving race cars, driving styles will always be a factor.

But is one style more likely to be the best in most situations? We could spend years discussing and arguing which style is ultimately going to lead to the best lap time, or the best race pace (which don't always go together, which is one of the reasons this discussion is so controversial and difficult to resolve). The answer is, in my opinion, not likely. Whatever style your driver finds most natural, and is most comfortable with, is going to be the most effective for him. Sure, it may not be perfect for every corner, but if he works to maximize his style, it will work best in most corners. Driving a race car is, after all, a series of compromises.

The important point is for you to recognize and understand your driver's style. To ask your driver to change his style completely to suit the car may not be very effective. Sure, it is important for your driver to adapt to the car's handling problems in a race (I'll talk more about this in Chapter 9). But there is a significant difference between adapting to the car and a wholesale change in driving style. That would be like forcing Shaquille O'Neal to only shoot three-pointers (or free throws!), or Tiger Woods to play more conservative shots. Yes, they could do it, but they would not be as effective.

There may be times that you would like your driver to use a different style, one that suited the car's handling better. Is telling him to change his style going to work? You know the answer to that question is no. To make any change, he has to change his programming, and that may take a bit of time—time that may be better used to change the car to suit his style.

I'm not saying that you should always change the car to suit your driver. What I am saying is that there are situations when it will be more time-effective to do that.

## Braking Strategies

Ask your driver what he would do, driving technique-wise, if he had to shave half a second off his lap time. If he is like most drivers, his first response would be to brake later for each corner. That would be his first priority. The problem is that even if he could brake later for each and every corner on a typical 2.5-mile road racing circuit, he would not gain half a second. Even if he braked significantly deeper, on most tracks he would gain less than a tenth or two.

So what would be a better strategy for trying to shave a serious amount of time off his lap? I suggest using a two-step approach:

1. Lighter braking: One of the problems with just braking later, other than it does not provide a big gain, is that it puts a lot of mental stress on your driver. If he has decided to brake later for a corner, when he approaches it there is a good chance that he will not brake efficiently. Instead, due to the stress and fear of trying to drive the car deeper into the corner, when he does hit the brake he will "hit" the brake. In other words, he will be waiting, waiting, waiting . . . and then slam down on the pedal. At that point, there is a good chance he will lock up the brakes and totally mess up the corner. And if he doesn't actually lock up the brakes, he will at least stand the car on its nose, upsetting the balance, and not gain anything. The reason, of course, is he is trying to enter the turn at the same speed as always.

If, instead, he began his braking at the same spot as usual, only lighter, he would end up carrying more speed into the corner. If he carried just 1 mile per hour more into each turn, he would get his half second.

2. Later braking: Once a driver has gotten comfortable braking a little lighter and carrying more speed into the corner(s), then he can start to brake later and harder again. Using this approach, he is more likely to brake accurately and achieve the ultimate goal of shaving more than a half second off his lap time.

When your driver has the goal of braking later for a corner, suggest to him that he use this two-step approach. First, brake at the same place but a little lighter (which builds his confidence and comfort level), and then brake later. Guaranteed, he will get to braking later much sooner, and with less grief (maybe even less damage to the car), than if he just went straight to trying to brake later.

## Fast Corner Strategy

Whether on a road course or an oval, perhaps the most difficult corner for any race driver is the very fast one—the one that can ultimately be taken flat out. The biggest problem for most drivers is that the self-preservation program in the right foot (at least that is where it seems to be!) takes control, causing it to lift off the throttle. As soon as that happens, the balance of the car is not ideal and now it feels as though it is on the limit. And, it may just be. Of course, it is the lift of the throttle that causes the car to be at the limit. If the driver had kept his foot flat to the floor, the car would have been better balanced, and it would have stuck—at the limit—through the corner.

In this situation, it is as if the driver's right foot has a mind of its own. And, rather than just telling your driver to keep his foot flat to the floor, or for him to tell himself that, he needs a better strategy than that.

The strategy is simple. Have your driver lift off the throttle early, well before turning into the corner, and then go back to full throttle before turn-in. This way, he will feel comfortable entering the corner at full throttle because the car will be going slow enough. And since he is now driving through the corner flat to the floor, the car will be balanced, telling him it has lots of grip, building his confidence. Therefore, the next lap he will feel comfortable lifting off the throttle a little less on the straightaway; the next lap lifting even less; and so on until he is completely flat through the corner.

It may sound as though this strategy takes more time, but in reality it doesn't. From my experience, both using it myself and coaching other drivers with it, your driver will be taking the corner flat out much sooner than if he just kept telling himself to take it flat.

The key is in building and maintaining your driver's comfort level. Without that, he will never take the corner at full throttle.

## Understeer-Oversteer Problem

How many times has your driver complained about the race car understeering early in a corner, and oversteering toward the exit? I don't know of a driver that has not driven a race car at some point in his career that does this. If they haven't yet, it is only a matter of time before they do.

*A car's oversteer is often actually caused by understeer earlier in the corner. Your job is to help your driver become aware if he is causing the oversteer by how he responds to corner-entry understeer.* Kent Regan

If your job is to engineer the car—to get rid of this early-understeer, late-oversteer problem—you know it is difficult. After all, the cure for half the problem often exaggerates the other half.

The biggest problem—the real problem—is that the problem is not always the fault of the car. The problem often lies with the driver. Of course, telling the driver he's the cause of the early-understeer, late-oversteer problem may result in a breakdown in communication at best!

The solution? Ask the driver some awareness-building questions. A common cause of this handling problem is that as the driver experiences understeer early in the corner, he turns the steering wheel even more. Think about it—put yourself in his place. You're entering a corner at 100 mph, you turn the steering wheel, and the car pushes toward the outside edge of the track. What would you do? Probably the same as many race drivers do: crank in more steering angle, trying to get it to turn. It is human instinct. It is survival instinct.

If you ask your driver exactly what he is doing when the understeer occurs, you begin the awareness-building process. Ask, "What position do you have the steering wheel in when the understeer occurs?" Give him time to think about it. Ask him to close his eyes and visualize what was happening.

If you ask him if he turns the steering wheel more, he may answer "no." He knows that is the "right" answer. Ask questions that will draw out the truth. And don't be in a hurry for the answer. Let him think it through—preferably visualizing what he had been doing.

A driver in this situation will become aware of the fact that he actually turns the steering wheel more when faced with the early-in-the-turn understeer. He will then realize that when he does that, it causes the oversteer later in the turn. What is happening, of course, is that as he turns the steering wheel more, the front tires begin to scrub off some speed, then suddenly regain traction, causing the car to snap to oversteer.

By simply becoming aware of what he is doing, as a result of your question, he has discovered the solution to the problem—not cranking in more steering input. Your next step is to help him develop his MI. Perhaps you could ask him what he should do, and how would that look, sound, and feel. Ask him to describe that to you in as much detail as possible. Ask him to close his eyes and imagine that in as much detail as possible; and to do that over and over again, daily, weekly, and monthly.

The key is defining the real cause of a problem. Many times the car is not the problem—the problem is the driver. Far too many teams have been led down the wrong path by not digging to the core of the problem; instead they chase the effects of the problem. Before you tweak away on the car's setup, raise the awareness of your driver to determine the real cause of a handling problem.

## Hustle

Areas where many drivers give up a lot of time are those very short sections of track where they think that part throttle is as much as the car can take—that it is "good enough"—when a short burst of full throttle is possible. Many drivers "coast" for a fraction of a second, thinking that 80 percent throttle is good enough. To me, they are not "hustling" the car.

Anything your driver can do that increases time he spends at full throttle is a good thing. Even if it's for a fraction of a second between two turns; or instead of slowly trailing off the throttle at the end of a straight he comes off the gas quickly (but smoothly). That's "hustling" the car.

I know this sounds obvious, but your driver's feet should either be on the brakes, squeezing the throttle down, or flat to the floor on the throttle.

Of course, just recognizing that he is not hustling the car is not enough, as easy as that is using data acquisition. Neither is telling him to hustle the car—to use full throttle in a few key parts of the track. Often, that just frustrates your driver by pointing out his weaknesses. This really is a place to use the learning formula. Have him get a clear MI, and then become aware of how close he is to this ideal MI by rating his own level of hustle on a scale of 1 to 10.

As he rates his hustle level, it will naturally progress from a 1 or 2 to at least an 8 over a short period of time—as long as he has spent the time to get a good clear MI in his mind. Going from 8 to 9 and then 10, the last couple of hundredths, may take a little longer, but will happen.

## Skid Pad Training

It amazes me how much time and money race teams spend on testing and developing their cars, and how little is spent on developing the driver. When was the last time your driver was on a skid pad? If you answered "never," you are not alone. If you answered "not in the past year," again you are in the majority. Very few drivers spend time developing and fine-tuning their abilities on a skid pad.

You owe it to your driver, your team, and yourself to get your driver onto a skid pad now. For most drivers there are three primary goals for a skid pad session:

- Learning/perfecting how to deal with understeer;
- Learning/perfecting how to steer the car with the throttle; and
- Knowing how the car reacts when going beyond the limit.

Ideally, your driver would drive his own race car on the skid pad, to feel what it will do when it reaches the limit, but that is not always practical. If your driver races an open-wheel car, for example, although it would be best if he could actually use it on the skid pad, using a production car will suffice. That is if the production car is a rear-wheel-drive, preferably with some form of limited slip differential. If your driver races a front-drive car, however, it is obviously better to use a similar car.

The good news is you really don't need a specific-built skid pad for this exercise. A large, relatively smooth, unobstructed, paved parking lot will do, as long as you can wet it down. The size of the driving area depends on the type of car being used, and how much room there is for error around the outside. In other words, area surrounded by fence may not be ideal, whereas the same area with grass or gravel all around it would be okay. Adding water is relatively easy, for all you need to do is have access to a fire hydrant, or just rent a water truck for a few hours.

It is best if you can place at least eight plastic cones around an inner circle. That is the inner boundary for your driver to drive around. Once you've wetted down the surface, it's time for your driver to go for a "spin."

The choice of whether to use slicks or wet tires is up to you, the size of the skid pad area, and the speed you want your driver to work at. You may even want to place wet tires on the front and slicks on the

*Drivers at all levels should spend time on a skid pad to fine-tune their car control skills. It is the most overlooked driver development tool.*
Gerry Frechette

rear to help induce oversteer, and vice versa. This is especially useful if the skid pad area is relatively small.

My usual routine for a driver is to have him initially go onto the skid pad just to get used to the amount of traction available. At this stage, he is beginning to learn how the car reacts when it goes beyond the limit. Have him drive the circle in both directions, making sure that he drives fast enough to make the car slide. If you do not have radio communications with your driver, work out some form of hand signal for when you want him to stop so you two can talk.

Once he has gotten a basic feel for it, the next objective is for him to work on correcting and controlling an understeering car. Ask him to increase his speed until the front tires begin to slide. You may have to make some adjustments to the car to ensure that it understeers. You want him to experience the understeer for at least one-third of the distance around the circle, and then have him correct it by reducing the amount of steering input slightly.

The goal is for him to experience how straightening the steering slightly controls the understeer. Most drivers know this is the correct technique at the intellectual or conscious level. If you ask your driver how to control excessive understeer, he will probably tell you that you should straighten the front wheels slightly (along with easing off the throttle). However, many drivers, until they have truly experienced this at a speed (and for a long enough time) where they can actually notice it, do not make the appropriate correction. In other words, it is not a subconscious program for them to straighten the steering wheel when faced with understeer. Instead, they actually turn the steering wheel even more, making the understeer worse. That is human instinct.

Have your driver practice inducing understeer, and then correcting it with the steering wheel, and the throttle. Have him do this over and over again. How many times? That's up to you and him. I've never met a race driver yet who didn't want to continue doing this until they were almost ready to get sick from going in circles. You want him to do it until correcting the understeer the appropriate way becomes habit—a subconscious program.

Then it is time to move on to oversteer, and particularly steering the car with the throttle. Again, you may have to make some slight adjustments to the car to make it a little easier for your driver to get the car to oversteer. However, he should be able to induce some power oversteer (obviously in a rear-wheel-drive car) with the throttle, and then be able to keep the car in a power-induced drift all the way around the circle for a number of laps. If he immediately spins the car, or cannot make it a lap around the circle without looping the car, you know he needs more practice.

Your driver should be able to keep the car in a drift, steering the car with the throttle as much as or more than with the steering wheel for at least a half-dozen laps or more. His throttle control, and his ability to drive the car at the limit without going too far beyond will greatly improve with this exercise.

Finally, have your driver go back onto the skid pad and just play. Have him induce some understeer and then correct it, induce oversteer and hold it there for a while, spin the car back in the other direction and do it all over again. The ability to induce the understeer and oversteer is just as important as knowing how to correct it. It should be a part of his overall awareness of how to control the car at its limit—and beyond.

Again, make sure he can do all of these exercises equally well in both directions around the circle.

## SPEED SECRET #27
### Skid pad training should be mandatory for your driver.

As I said, I've never met a true race driver who did not truly enjoy spending a couple of hours on a skid pad. And I've never seen one who didn't benefit greatly from the experience. By the way, this should not be a once-in-a-lifetime experience. The more your driver does this, no matter what level he is currently at, the better he will be. I know of current Champ Car drivers who would benefit tremendously from this exercise.

### Driver's Perception

One of the most entertaining but confusing conversations you can ever listen in on is one between a couple of drivers discussing where they begin braking for a corner. There are times when you may begin to wonder if they are actually talking about the same corner. The reason for this is simple. Different people perceive things differently.

This explains why one driver will claim to brake at the 200 marker, while the other says he drives the car all the way into the 150, all the while the data acquisition would show they both brake at the exact spot. So which one is telling the truth? Both. It is just that what one driver sees as braking at 200, the other sees as 150.

It can sometimes be explained as simply as one driver beginning to brake when his car is passing the 200 marker, while the other driver begins braking when the 150 marker lines up with the front of the car in his vision (which is well before the car passes it).

This obviously applies to far more than braking points. Simply suggesting to your driver to apex a corner "at the end of the curb where other drivers do" may not get the result you are looking for. He may think—perceive—that he is already doing that. This is why raising your driver's awareness level is so critical.

For example, if you observe your driver apexing before the end of the curbing, and you think he needs to apex at the end of the curbing, just telling him to apex there will not help. Instead, ask him "Where are you apexing now?" and no matter what his reply is, ask him to try apexing 2 feet later. Without asking him to become aware of where he is apexing now, he really has no way of knowing exactly what he needs to change.

## Street Driving

Does your driver spend more time behind the wheel of his street car or his race car? My bet is on the street car (if he is old enough to have a license). I would also bet that he develops many of his bad driving habits—bad programming—while driving on the street. If you want your driver to perform well on the track, you must help him become aware of how his street driving affects his racetrack performance, and of any bad habits he is programming on the street.

Making him aware of any bad street driving habits may be more of a challenge than engineering his race driving. After all, few race drivers take criticism of their driving habits well. That is why it is important to find a way of making him aware of the bad habits without it sounding like you are telling him how to drive.

The best way to start, obviously, is by helping him become aware of how important his street driving techniques are to the physical programming of his race driving. Ask him to begin to think about that, and to compare how much time he spends driving on the street to the time spent behind the wheel of his race car. Ask him to imagine how smoothly and skilled he thinks Michael Schumacher drives on the street, and to model him.

I would also recommend that he read *Jackie Stewart's Principles of Performance Driving*. Stewart, besides being one of the greatest race drivers of all time, truly understood the relationship between driving on the racetrack and the street.

## Why Drivers Do What They Do

Here's an example of a conversation I've had more than once with the car engineer of the team where I'm coaching the driver.

Car Engineer: "Look at the data. He's braking way early for turn 1. You need to do something with him."

Coach: "Yes, that's exactly what I saw when I was watching the last practice. But I'm not sure if the problem lies entirely with him. He normally brakes very late."

Car Engineer: "Yes, but look at him now. What's wrong with him?"

Coach: "Again, I'm not sure if it's him. He's like most other drivers I've worked with—he only does something different if the car has 'told' him to do something different. For some reason he is sensing that he needs to brake earlier for turn 1. Often, drivers are not even totally aware that they are doing this—that the car has told them to do something different, or not to drive it at what seems to us to be the limit. What we need to do is help him become aware of why he is doing this. We need to help him figure out what the car is doing to tell him to brake early. Obviously, nothing he said in our debrief indicated a problem, but let's call him back in for another talk."

Driver comes in.

Coach: "Car Engineer and I have been looking over the data and it's got us thinking about how we can improve the car."

Driver: "Great!"

Coach: "Approaching turn 1, where do you begin braking?"

Driver: "At the 3 marker."

Coach: "How does the car feel there?"

Driver: "Ahh . . . Well, a couple of other cars I ran with in that last session seemed to brake a bit later than me. . . ."

Coach: "But how did the car feel? Is it stable under braking? Does it stop well? How's the brake pedal feel?"

Driver: "The pedal's good. It seems to stop okay, and it's not moving around on me—it's stable."

Coach: "How about at turn-in? How does it feel there?"

Driver (closing his eyes and imagining what it was like): "Now that I think about it, the car gets loose at turn-in."

Coach: "Are you completely off the brakes at the point it begins to oversteer, or just trailing off?"

Driver: "It's just as I trail off the brakes while turning in—it's nervous there. I feel like it's going to swap ends if I turn the wheel too quickly."

Coach: "If the car felt more stable—had less turn-in oversteer—what would that do to your braking?"

Driver: "Well, I could probably carry a little more speed into the corner, so I could easily brake later—probably close to the 2.5 marker."

Car Engineer: "So it's initial turn-in oversteer? Does it feel like the rear of the car is falling over, or just sliding too much?"

Driver: "I think the rear is falling over—it feels like it's moving around too much."

Car Engineer: "Okay, I can change that with a shock adjustment—slow the rear roll down a bit by increasing the rear rebound. Do you want to try that for the next session?"

Driver: "Yes. If you can make it less nervous at turn-in, I can brake later and carry more speed into turn 1. I'll feel more confident there—I can do a better job. It will probably help in turns 5 and 7 as well."

Rarely do drivers with a little experience do something wrong or not drive the car near the limit for no reason at all. Most times it's because the car is telling them to do so. And as this example demonstrates, the problem is not always where it first appears. The real problem was not that the car had a braking problem. It was a problem later on—corner turn-in—that made the driver react earlier on.

### SPEED SECRET #28
### Drivers do what they do most often because the car "told" them to.

I can't tell you the number of times I've had conversations just like this one. Perhaps the best part of this example—and it does happen like this with the right approach—is that no one felt threatened. There was no blame being put on anyone. The car engineer was simply looking for answers, not to blame the driver. And the driver admitted he could do a better job if the car made him felt more confident.

And the key ingredient to solving this problem? Once again, awareness. First of all, the data acquisition helped the car engineer become aware of an area where improvements could be made. Then, by asking a number of questions, the driver became more aware, and could then provide the information the car engineer required to improve the car.

Any time you see an area where your driver could improve, ask the question, "What's making him do what he's doing?" Most times, the car is telling him to do it. Then, by asking some questions, you can raise the awareness of both of you, and you will find the answers.

# Chapter 7

# Team Dynamics

Is auto racing a team sport or an individual sport? I know some race drivers act as though it is entirely an individual sport, but it is definitely a team sport. Having said that, once your driver is in the race, barring pit stops, it is an individual sport. Sure, it took a team to get him there, but at that point it is totally up to the driver. Or is it? The team dynamics, the energy level within the team, the communication, and the ability of team members to work together are the deciding factors in how well the driver performs in the race.

Looking at the history of auto racing, there have been many great dynamic duos; a combination of driver and engineer/team manager that has won more than their fair share of races and championships. Colin Chapman and Jim Clark, Colin Chapman and Mario Andretti, Roger Penske and Mark Donahue, Roger Penske and Rick Mears, Ross Brawn and Michael Schumacher, Steve Challis and Greg Moore, Mo Nunn and Alex Zanardi, Mo Nunn and Juan Montoya, Ray Evernham and Jeff Gordon are just a few of the greatest "teams." I don't think the fact that Colin Chapman, Roger Penske and Mo Nunn are each mentioned twice is simply coincidence. These legendary team owners/ managers/engineers knew and know how to communicate with drivers. In fact, that may be the key to them becoming legendary.

## Communication

Communication may just be the most important factor in a successful driver-engineer relationship. I don't know of any driver coach who can read his driver's mind, and vice versa. You must understand your driver's preferred learning style, and he yours, as this is the basis of good

121

communications. You need to talk about how you communicate best. And more important, you need to listen. By doing that enough, it will begin to seem as though you and your driver can read each other's minds.

### SPEED SECRET #29
### The driver engineer may need to play facilitator to enhance communications between driver and team.

By listening to your driver, you can learn a lot. If you ask him to describe how the car reacts to a change, or what feedback the car is giving him, you can learn more than just what the car is doing. You can discover the keys to good communication with him.

*The key to success with any team is communication. Part of driver engineering is helping to facilitate communication between your driver and the rest of the team.*

For example, if you ask your driver to give you feedback on what the car is doing in a particular corner, and his response is something along the lines of, "It sounds like I'm getting too much wheelspin off the turn," or "I can hear the tires scrubbing off speed through the fast sweeper," you know that auditory input is very important to him. If he is a kinesthetic learner, his response is more likely to be focused on what he felt, i.e., "It feels like I'm getting some wheelspin coming off the corner." A visual learner will talk more about what he sees.

You may also be able to pick up some of this knowledge by listening to the way he talks in regular conversations. A visual processor will use phrases such as "I see what you mean"; a kinesthetic learner might say "I know how you feel"; and an auditory learner say "I hear what you are saying," or "listen here." By paying attention to the words and phrases your driver uses, you can pick up on these subtleties that can lead to the communication level that wins championships.

The problem with some engineers is that they only hear what they want to hear. And they only want to hear what the car is doing, while that is not enough to also engineer the driver. You need to practice listening to your driver. At the same time, you need to educate your driver in how to listen to you—and how to communicate with you. Again, I doubt whether he can read your mind. So you may have to tell him how to communicate with you.

If you want him to tell you what the car is doing, because you are an auditory processor, then tell him. If you are a visual processor, then tell him to draw or write out what the car is doing. And if you are a kinesthetic processor, have him show you what the car is doing, even if that means driving the track in a street car or using a model to demonstrate the attitude of the car.

How do you know how to help your driver get in his performance state of mind prior to a qualifying session or race? Start by asking him. Does he want you to "push" him, or calm him down? Does he want you to talk to him right up to the moment he drives off, or does he like to be left alone?

One sure way of destroying your ability to work with your driver is to be unclear about what you expect of him, and he of you. In other words, to be unclear as to the roles and responsibilities, whether that be yours or his. If you expect him to get out of the car, give you feed-back on the car, and then get out of the way, then tell him. If you want him to hang around, help with team morale, or to be available for more debriefing, let him know. More potentially great relationships have been ruined by misunderstandings about what was expected of the driver than just about anything else. And again, the opposite is true. Make sure you know what your driver expects of you.

You may have already figured out that the key to all this is just plain, old-fashioned conversation. The more you talk and listen to your driver, the better you will understand each other.

## Personality Traits

If you think back to the discussion in Chapter 2 on personality traits, and specifically on what the behavioral profiles of you and your driver look like, you may begin to see where problems could occur.

For example, let's say your driver has a high level of dominance, is very outgoing, not so patient, and couldn't care less about details. At the same time, being dominant is not so important to you, you are more introverted and patient, and details are everything. Can you see where a potential clash could occur? Trying to extract the details of how the car is performing is like pulling teeth. He wants the car to be dead-on perfect, right now, not by the time qualifying comes around. When you want a one-on-one debriefing with him, he is out chatting with friends, competitors, or just about anyone else who will listen. And he wants to be in control of the decisions about the car setup, the team, what hotel the crew is staying in, where dinner is going to be tonight . . . and so on.

And that is just your and his behavior. Now, mix in the rest of the race team.

How big a problem is this? As big as you let it become. Can you change your personality traits, or those of your driver? Yes, you can, through mental programming. And that is something you may have to help your driver do if both of you agree that dialing up or down on one or more of these traits will make him a better race driver.

But within a team environment, the most important factor is not necessarily making changes to people's traits, it is being aware and understanding them. If, for example, you know your driver's patience level, and he knows yours, it makes it much easier to work together and actually complement each other.

You could have each member of your team profiled using one of the professional firms or software packages, such as PDP or Meyers-Briggs. However, that is probably not necessary for your purposes. If you simply have each member of your team do a self-evaluation, using a chart similar to the one on this page, it will provide you with what you need. Make sure that each person doing the self-evaluation fully understands what each of the traits really mean. Go back to Chapter 2 for the details. In each category—dominance, extroversion, pace/patience, and conformity—have each team member rate them-selves, placing a mark on the scale that represents where they see themselves.

After everyone has completed the chart, sit down together and talk through each person's profile. The objective is twofold. One, after some

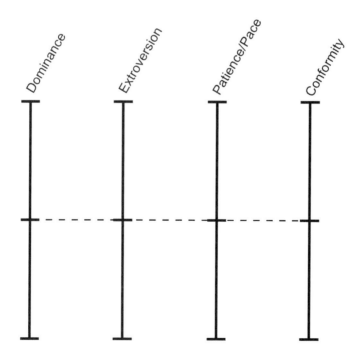

input from other people, a person may need to adjust where they are on the scale slightly. And two, it is as important—or even more—for everyone to know what each other's profile looks like.

The key to the success of this is in the doing of the exercise. It creates an awareness and understanding for everyone involved of why individuals behave the way they do, and how to manage each other in the most effective way with this information in mind.

### Team Energy

I'm sure you have had the experience of one person joining a group of people, and the energy from that person bringing everyone either up or down. It's amazing the impact just one person can have on a group of people. More important, it's amazing what impact just one person can have on the performance of your driver. That one person may or may not be you.

If there is a person around your driver who could have a negative impact on your driver's energy—and therefore his performance—that person needs to be separated from the driver. Of course, this becomes very delicate when that person is a family member or close friend. If it is a crew member, it may be in the best interests of the team to remove him from the team.

### SPEED SECRET #30
### Encourage and build team energy.

In practically any close working relationship, one person will mirror the other to some extent. This certainly occurs when engineering a driver. If you show any level of frustration with your driver's performance, he will as well. If you are confident in his ability to perform, he will be too.

# Chapter 8

# Data Acquisition

I have no intention of talking about the technical side of data acquisition systems. What I want to discuss in this chapter is how to use them to help engineer the driver.

The first and most important point is that no data acquisition system in the world, no matter how sophisticated, can ever replace your driver's feedback. The most successful car engineers know this as fact. They know that given the option of taking the input from the data acquisition system or from the driver, the driver's feedback is more important.

Am I saying a driver's feedback is more accurate than data acquisition? No, I'm not. What I'm saying is that no matter what the data says, if the driver feels, reads, or perceives the car in another way, that is the way it is. The old saying, "perception is reality" definitely applies in the case of race drivers.

If you want to know a sure way of de-motivating your driver, tell him you trust and value the information gathered from the data acquisition system more than his feedback. And with most drivers, you don't have to come right out and say that—they can read that in you.

So from this you might begin to think that I do not have much use for data acquisition systems on race cars. You couldn't be farther from the truth. They are one of the most important tools a driver engineer can use. When I'm engineering a driver, I almost demand the car has data acquisition. And the most successful car engineers know that data acquisition is an extremely valuable tool to not only engineer the car, but also to engineer the driver.

*Use data acquisition to enhance and confirm*
*your driver's feedback.*

## Synchronizing the Driver to the Data Acquisition System

The first step in using data acquisition in engineering your driver is to synchronize the two. Without doing this, the data acquisition system and your driver will often not agree, and that can only lead to problems.

What do I mean by synchronizing the two? I mean training the driver to read the track and car in a way that matches what the data acquisition system says. I also mean learning to interpret the data in

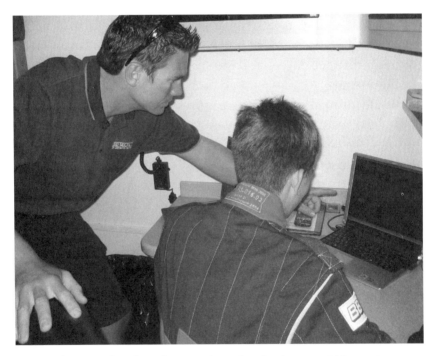

*Your driver needs to learn how to relate what the data acquisition system says to the feel he has from the actual driving. With enough experience, he will be able to predict what the data looks like based on what he felt when driving, and vice versa. This can speed up debriefs and make them much more accurate.*

a way that matches what the driver is reporting. When that happens, you can make great gains in the performance of both your driver and the car.

Am I saying that the driver and data acquisition must always agree? No. There is nothing wrong with seeing two sides of the story: how the driver feels, reads, and perceives it; and how the data acquisition reports it. The information you require to make the car perform better is in the feedback coming from the two sources.

I talked about this earlier, but I'll mention it again. Many times you may be able to make the race car faster, but it will become less comfortable for the driver. An uncomfortable driver is a slow driver. Sometimes the data is telling you to make one change—one that would ultimately make the car quicker—and the driver is telling you to make a change that will result in a more comfortable, confidence-inspiring car. Nine times out of ten, going with what the driver wants will result in the biggest improvement in performance of the driver/car package.

You may be thinking to yourself, "It's obvious this book is written by a driver! He's always taking the driver's side." And, obviously it is. However, I've engineered and coached enough drivers, worked with enough car engineers, and engineered enough cars to have seen this from the outside. And, as a driver, I've also seen it from the inside.

You can never lose sight of the fact that we don't race cars without drivers, and drivers don't race without cars. It is a package, one whose overall performance is not dictated by just one part of it. The car/driver package's performance is limited by the weakest half. But only one half of the package is human. The human element is likely to be the most challenging component.

## Reading and Interpreting the Data

While I don't intend to get into any type of discussion as to how to interpret data from a car engineering point of view, I want to touch on a few areas that relate strictly to the driver. What I hope to do is help you become aware of a few tendencies to keep an eye on, as they can tell you a lot about your driver.

## Throttle–Brake-Throttle Transition

One of the most obvious driving traits identifiable with data acquisition is what your driver is doing with the throttle and brakes from the end of a straightaway through the exit of a corner. The common things to look for are

- Lifting off the throttle and coasting before applying the brakes,
- Releasing the brakes too suddenly,
- Too long a gap between full release of the brakes and application of the throttle, and
- Too abrupt on the application of the throttle.

Look for a smooth, seamless overlap of braking and throttle, in both directions: from throttle to brake, and brake to throttle. If there is any gap between the two, your driver is wasting time. If the application or releasing of either the brakes or the throttle is too abrupt, he

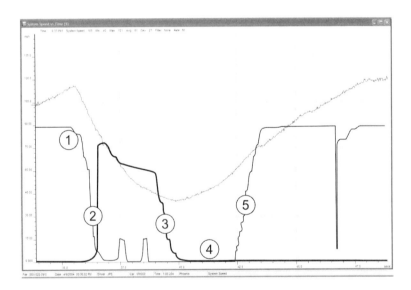

*This data trace demonstrates a number of problems: (1) The driver eased off the throttle (the medium thick line) too slowly and gently; (2) there's too long a gap between coming off the throttle and the beginning of braking (the thick line); (3) the driver didn't trail off the brakes gently enough; (4) there's too long a gap between the end of braking and the beginning of acceleration; and (5), the application of the throttle is too abrupt.*

will not be smooth enough to be really fast; if it is too slow and gradual, he will be too slow.

## Braking Forces

Watch for inconsistent braking forces. Typically, braking forces should ramp up very quickly, stay consistent at the limit, and then trail off smoothly. Some drivers initially stand on the brakes, and then begin to ease off, while others do the opposite—they take a long time to squeeze full pressure on the pedal, only getting to maximum threshold braking at the very end, just prior to turning in to the corner.

You need to consider the type and performance of the car your driver is driving. If the car has a lot of aerodynamic downforce, then the initial application of the brakes should be very hard and quick. From there, the driver should begin to trail off some pressure as the car's traction is reduced as the downforce is reduced with less and less speed.

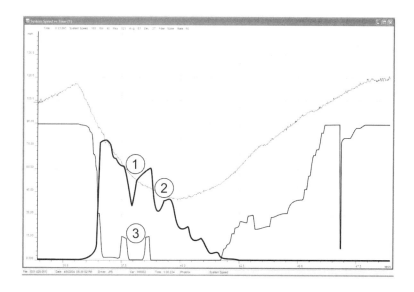

*The braking trace (the thick line) in this graph shows the driver applying inconsistent braking forces (at 1 and 2). In this case, with each downshifting blip of the throttle (3) there is a reduction in braking force.*

If the car has little to no aerodynamic downforce, the braking should be relatively consistent all the way through the braking zone. The only reason your driver should alter the pressure through the length of the braking zone is variations in the track surface, and therefore the grip level of the track. If the braking zone is flat and smooth, so should the brake pressure trace on the data acquisition.

### Steering Inputs

Often, you can detect a lack of driver confidence by studying the steering input trace. For example, a driver who is not confident with what his car will do when he turns into a corner—perhaps fearing it will oversteer immediately or understeer—will turn the wheel too gradually, instead of turning it accurately and crisply. He will begin turning the steering wheel prior to the ideal turn-in point, progressively turning the wheel too slowly.

If you compare and synchronize what your driver reports to you (his awareness), what your observations are (your awareness), and the data trace (the computer's awareness), over time you will learn to recognize a lack of driver confidence in the car. Obviously, this is invaluable information, as it is not until you've identified a problem that you can find the cause and its cure.

### Throttle Histogram

Many drivers and engineers use the throttle histogram to determine whether a change to the car or driving technique resulted in a positive or negative change. The thinking is that if the driver is able to spend more time at full throttle—a greater percentage of the lap with the throttle flat to the floor—then that is an improvement.

While I would agree with this where one driver's lap is compared to his own previous laps, I want to warn you about going too far with it. It is possible to be at full throttle for a greater percentage of a lap, and still be slower. How? By also spending much more time at no throttle—with no throttle applied whatsoever, perhaps even while braking.

When you compare the percentage of lap spent at full throttle, also compare how much of the lap is spent with no throttle applied. A 1 percent increase in the amount of lap spent at full throttle will not

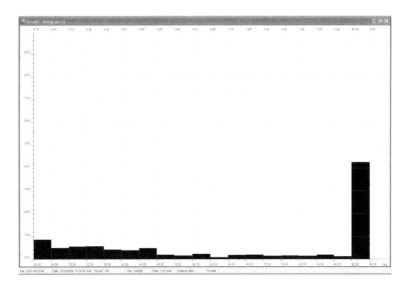

*The throttle histogram is a useful tool to determine whether a change in car setup or driving technique results in more time spent at full throttle. But be aware of reading too much into the information, as an increase in time spent at full throttle along with a reduction in time spent at part throttle could actually result in a slower lap time.*

result in a faster lap time if the driver also spends 5 percent more time completely off the throttle.

Also, if you are comparing more than one driver using the throttle histogram, understand that driving style is a big factor. Some drivers are either on or off the throttle; while others spend less overall time at full throttle, and are still quicker, since they spend more time squeezing the throttle down in the mid-range.

The best way to use the throttle histogram is to compare the average percent throttle. In this case, more is always better, since you are comparing the total amount of time your driver is on the throttle.

### Theoretical Fastest Lap

Most quality data acquisition systems have the capability to produce a report after a session that predicts your driver's theoretical fastest lap. It does this by adding up the fastest times from each segment of the track throughout the session.

133

Although the lap time the system predicts can sometimes be a bit unrealistic, with enough laps to pick and choose from, it is a great way to evaluate how consistent your driver is. If the spread between his best lap time from the session and the theoretical fastest lap is less than 1 percent, that's a sign of a driver who can consistently get the most out of the car (unless he is just plain slow, in which case he is just not using the full limits of the car). If it is much more than that, there must be some reason for his inconsistency: either he is experimenting with his driving technique, he is not confident in what the car is doing and telling him, or he made an error on one or more laps that skewed the data.

# Chapter 9

# The Role of Testing and Practice

For most, if not all, engineers, crew chiefs, mechanics, team owners, team managers, and even drivers themselves, testing and practice is for one thing: developing the race car. I suggest that is only part of its role. In addition to developing the car, testing and practice should also develop the driver. In fact, you should really look at it as developing the car-driver package.

### SPEED SECRET #32
**Use testing to develop the driver as much as to develop the car.**

### Developing Sensitivity

How important is it for your driver to be sensitive to any and all subtle changes made to the car? You can either hope your driver has the necessary sensitivity, or you can help him develop it. A big part of testing and practice should be used to develop his sensitivity.

As I mentioned earlier, one of the most effective tools you can use to improve the performance of your driver, and his sensitivity to setup changes, are sensory input and traction sensing sessions. You may be thinking that track time, whether on a private test day or during an event practice session, is far too valuable to be spent

135

on training the driver. And you are right . . . if you have no interest in winning.

If you do want to win, then one of the reasons practice and testing is so valuable is the opportunity to improve the car-driver package. That means developing the driver just as much as you develop the car.

If you need more convincing, think of it this way. The better your driver gets at soaking up sensory inputs, the better his feedback will be about the car. I'm sure you will agree, without good feedback from your driver, you cannot do what it takes to maximize the race car. You need his feedback to do your job properly.

## Learning

Rarely does a team go to a track for a race and have to be on the pace right out of the box. While that would be nice, at most events there are one or more practice sessions prior to qualifying and the race. So think about it. When does your car and driver have to be as fast as they can possibly go? For one lap of qualifying, and then in the race, right?

Use the practice sessions for learning—learning how to be as fast as possible for your qualifying lap and for the race. This strategy provides better results in the race.

If at all possible during a test day, try to end the day on a positive note. People tend to recall most vividly the last piece of information they had. This is referred to as the "recency effect," meaning that what was most recent is now most deeply programmed into the brain. In other words, your driver will recall and mentally replay his last session on the track more than any other. Mentally recalling and replaying creates programming. I'm sure you would rather he programmed a technically correct, positive experience than the opposite.

This also suggests how important it is that you recognize when your driver starts to become tired, either physically or mentally, so that you can stop him before he begins programming errors. Remember, practice does not create perfect—only perfect practice creates perfect. It is far better to quit a test session early than have him practice, and get good at, making errors. Of course, if he is physically and/or mentally tired before the end of a test day, you need to help him create a fitness training program that will ensure it doesn't happen again.

## Adaptability

Certainly, there are times you want your driver to drive the car in the exact same way as he has in the past. Without consistency it is difficult, if not impossible, to determine if changes to the car's setup helped or hindered. That is what being a good test driver is all about.

But there are times when it is important for your driver to adapt to whatever the car is doing. That is what being a good racer is all about. For example, if the car develops a turn-in understeer in the middle of the race, you had better hope that your driver knows how to adapt to it, otherwise you are going to have to watch him go backward in the pack.

How many times have you heard a driver complain about how his "car began to push in the middle of the race"? More than once, I would bet. But how often have you heard that same driver follow up that statement with, "and I didn't know what to do about it"? Never. And yet, it's often the case.

How does your driver develop the necessary adaptability? By educating him on the dynamics of the car, and giving him the time and opportunity to practice—to learn—during a test session.

The overall objective is for your driver to learn to be more adaptable to a car's handling problems. Most drivers try to force a bad handling car to do what they want it to do. That won't work. A driver can't make a car do what it doesn't want to do. The only option is to adapt to it.

To improve your driver's ability to adapt, spend a portion of a test day going through the following routine. Begin by allowing your driver to warm up and set a baseline with the car fairly neutral in its handling. Then work on adapting to understeer. Tune the car's setup to make the car understeer during the entry to the corners, the mid-corner phase, and while exiting the turns. Then have your driver try adapting—lessening the negative effects of the understeer. Give him time to play with different turn-in points and techniques, varying the amount of trail braking, and so on.

After that, have him work on adapting to oversteer by altering the line, changing the speed at which he turns in, when and where he releases the brakes and then gets back to power. For more details on how a driver can adapt to handling problems, see *Speed Secrets 2*.

The method your driver uses to adapt is dependent somewhat on where in the corner the understeer or oversteer begins, whether the car is in a steady state or transient state, and what your driver is doing to it. Therefore, when making the changes in the car's handling, try using the shocks, anti-roll bars, and maybe even springs and aerodynamics to vary the timing and severity of the handling problem.

In adapting, your driver needs to compare RPMs at a reference point on the straightaways as well as lap times to see which method works best. You may want to do that as well with the data acquisition information. One method may work in one type of corner but not another. And even though it may have helped in one corner, you might have lost at another part of the track, so the lap times will not tell the real story. That's why it is important to compare straightaway speeds as well as lap times.

Ultimately, which method works best does not matter. The main goal is for your driver to use any and all of the methods, for at some time any one will be the best choice. He should become aware of how to do each method, how it may or may not help, and what to expect from each one. This is all about adding information and knowledge to the data bank in his head.

Chapter 6 discusses driving style, and that there is not one style that suits every car and corner. Rather, a great driver will vary his style to suit the situation. One of the ways he learns how to do that is through practice, and this adaptability exercise is one of the best ways for a driver to learn to vary his style.

If you have time, as a complement to the above exercise, you might want to try another—one that shouldn't take too much time, but will be valuable as well. This time, starting with a balanced car, *your driver* (with his driving) makes the car understeer at entry, in the middle of the corner, and at the exit; and makes it oversteer at entry, mid-corner, and exit. The idea is if he knows how to make it do these things, he may recognize (become aware of) himself doing some little bit of this at some time—if he realizes he may be causing some of the understeer or oversteer, it becomes easy to fix.

Exactly how does he induce the understeer or oversteer with his driving? That is up to him to find out. He should experiment with how he turns the steering wheel (the timing, how abrupt or smooth, the speed at which he turns it, etc.), the cornering line, controlling the weight transfer (with the brakes and throttle), and the car's speed. If someone told him exactly what to do to make it understeer or oversteer, he would not get as much out of it. It is the experimenting—the trial and error, the self-discovery—that will help him become aware.

Deliberately making the car understeer or oversteer makes your driver aware of whether he is causing or exaggerating any handling problem. It is like a golfer who consistently slices his tee shots. The typical fix is to turn his body or change his grip to compensate for where the ball is likely to go. The best fix, though, is to go to a driving range and deliberately slice a number of balls. By figuring out how to make yourself slice the ball, you have identified how to fix the cause of the problem.

This approach uses the MI + A = G to the fullest extent, but at a subconscious level. Using this approach, most drivers will fix any problem without even trying. It seems ironic, perhaps, that by trying to make an error, your driver becomes aware of what causes the error, therefore allowing him to fix it.

## Practicing Q-Mode and R-Modes

It really is unfair to expect your driver to qualify at his best if he has not been allowed to practice it. With many cars and tire combinations requiring the driver to put in his perfect qualifying lap on a specific number of laps into a session, your driver's job becomes even more challenging.

The primary way for him to learn to qualify is through physical programming—practice. Yes, mental programming is also very important—and you must help him do that as well—but it is difficult to visualize something you have never, or rarely done. You must give him the time to experience it, and practice it. Then he should go away and mentally program driving in what I call Q-mode.

The combination of physical and mental programming of Q-mode will result in your driver putting your car in the grid position it deserves.

In addition to programming his Q-mode, he should also work on various R-modes. What do I mean? In most forms of racing, a driver is not necessarily going to drive the entire race at what is often referred to as ten-tenths. In *Speed Secrets 3: Inner Speed Secrets*, Ronn Langford and I defined that as R-1. R-2, on the other hand, is the mode where your driver is backed off just so very slightly, at a pace that he could maintain all day; R-1 is more of a "flyer" lap, most likely used in qualifying and the first and last few laps of a race. R-1 is on such a ragged edge that your driver would probably find it difficult to maintain throughout a race. R-3 is backed off from R-2 a bit more, and is perhaps used to save the tires, brakes, gearbox, or engine.

The important point here is that a driver cannot make the decision in the middle of a race to back off a bit, or to crank it back up again near the end of a race, without having a subconscious program to do that. I'm sure you have witnessed a driver who tried to back off slightly to protect a lead, only to crash. Or the driver who crashed, having had a big lead and being able to back off, only to have to crank it back up to the R-1 mode after a full course yellow ate up his lead. Even drivers such as Ayrton Senna and Michael Schumacher have made big errors trying to change modes at the conscious level.

These different levels, or modes, must be programmed. And, once again, the most effective way of programming them is through physical and mental practice. So you need not only to let your driver practice driving at the R-1, R-2, and R-3 levels, you need to help him trigger them. After some physical and mental programming, spend a session saying to your driver over the radio (or by pit board), R-1, R-2, or R-3, and have him immediately drive at that level.

### Building Programs

Perhaps the greatest hockey player of all time, Wayne Gretzky, said, "No matter who you are, no matter how good an athlete you are, we're creatures of habit. The better your habits, the better they'll be in pressure situations." One of the roles of practice is to build better habits, or better programming.

Of course, just practicing driving around a racetrack may not be the most efficient use of time. As I've said before, only perfect practice makes perfect, so any amount of track time your driver gets should be supervised and focused. If not, he may just get better at doing the wrong thing. And this applies no matter the driver's level.

It has always amazed me how the greatest athletes in any sport are generally credited with having superior natural talent, and yet they all seem to practice more, harder, and with more focus than their competitors. It makes me wonder if all that natural talent is really just more (and better) practice.

Michael Jordan would show up for a game before other members of his team to practice his shot. During a short period of time early in 2001 when Tiger Woods was not winning everything in sight, he claimed it was because he was working on shots he would need specifically for the Masters later that year. Some people doubted his claim . . . until he won the Masters again. Martina Navratilova, winner of 167 singles titles in tennis, including a record nine Wimbledons, said, "Every great shot you hit, you've hit a bunch of times in practice." And here we just thought it was all her natural talent that won those tournaments!

The stories of Michael Schumacher's commitment to practice and being the best are already part of his legend. After a day of testing at Ferrari's test track, where he has just completed the equivalent of two full Grand Prix race lengths, he will spend a couple of hours in the gym working out.

The point is that no athlete, not even your driver, can be expected to be the best if he doesn't practice, both on and off the track. That practice is all about building better programming. The more he builds better programming, the more people will credit him with natural talent.

# Chapter 10

# *The Inner Game*

If you didn't believe that being a successful race driver was more mental than physical before reading this book, I'm sure you now do. With that in mind, let me give you a few final thoughts.

## Competition Versus Performance

This may be one of the more difficult concepts for you and your driver to buy into. If you, your driver, and the whole team focuses their energies on enhancing the team's performance, rather than on competing, your chances of winning go up.

As I said in the introduction, in racing especially, most people typically rate their performance based on their result. For example, if your driver wins, you think of that as a great performance; and if he finishes in third, fifth, tenth, or anywhere other than winning, you think of that as a poor performance.

Is that the most accurate way of looking at performance? The problem is that most people in racing rate their performance based on the result, not the cause. What is the cause of winning, most times? Great performances, right? (Yes, others' misfortunes can play a role in the results.) What is the cause of not winning, most times? Less-than-great performances.

So rather than focus on the result, you, your driver, and team should focus on the cause—the performance. That often means focusing less on the competition and more on yourself. After all, you cannot do anything about the competition. You can only do something about yourself, your driver and your team.

I've seen it, and I bet you have too, where a driver or engineer spends massive amounts of time and energy looking at the competition.

If that driver or engineer had spent that same amount of time and energy on enhancing his own performance, the competition would have been so far behind there would have been no way they could have even seen them.

Whenever you focus on your competition, you tend to follow what they are doing. And the best you will ever do when following your competition is finish second.

Am I saying that winning is not important? No, I'm not! Winning is very important. But it is not the objective. The objective is to perform well—at the peak. When you do that, you are more likely to win. It's ironic, in fact. When you focus on winning, you are less likely to win. When you focus on your performance, and don't worry about winning, you are more likely to win.

## Pressure

How often does putting pressure on a person result in them performing better? Not often, right? And yet, many people in racing seem to do whatever they can to do just that to their driver.

There are two kinds of pressure: external and internal. Someone other than your driver applies external pressure; your driver applies the internal pressure. Rarely is external pressure beneficial to any driver. There are times when a driver has developed the mental programming where a certain amount of internal pressure results in better performance, but usually both internal and external pressure have the same negative effect.

One of your roles as driver engineer is to help control the pressure put on your driver. But does it help to simply tell your driver to not put pressure on himself, to not feel any pressure, or just say there is no pressure? No, it doesn't. In fact, it is impossible for him to not think about whatever is putting pressure on him. He can't *not* think about it.

Dealing with pressure is a two-step procedure, one that can be described in two words: *expectations* and *distraction*. Do away with the first, and use the second. If you keep this rule in mind, you will go a long way toward helping your driver handle the inevitable pressure.

Most of the pressure comes from expectations, so the first step is to do away with them. Understand, there is a significant difference

*Ultimately, the pressure on a driver comes from within, although the people around a driver can play a big role in it. By helping your driver focus on his performance—the act of driving—you can reduce the effects of the pressure on him.* Bruce Cleland between expectations and goals or objectives, with expectations being dangerous. Dangerous in what way? In a way that rarely leads to either a great performance, or the result (expectation) you or your driver want. All it does is generate pressure.

To me, the difference between expectations and goals and objectives is that the former has no direction. It is like saying, "I expect to be in New York City." That provides no direction, no incentive, no motivation, no purpose. But "my goal is to be in New York City" immediately begins the process of getting there. When you expect something, it removes the responsibility of how you are going to get it. When a person has a goal of achieving something, there is the responsibility of doing whatever it takes to make that goal a reality.

Expectations are solely focused on the result, while goals focus a person more on the performance it will take to achieve them. The first step, then, is to focus your driver on his performance so he forgets all about the pressure.

## SPEED SECRET #33
### Remove expectations by focusing on the possibilities.

The second step may be to distract his mind away from the pressure. The best way of doing this is to go back and look in your driver engineering toolbox. There you will find a couple of tools that, among other things, will distract his conscious mind away from the pressure to live up to some expectation. It is a tool that gets him focusing on a black race car, rather than a pink race car—what he wants to focus on, rather than what he doesn't want to focus on.

Perhaps the best tools to distract his mind from the pressure are the sensory input and traction sensing sessions. What you are doing is giving him a specific project that is easy for him to focus on, rather than on *not* focusing on the pressure. By asking your driver to focus on providing more detailed feedback on how the car feels, for example, it is practically impossible for him to focus on and feel the pressure. It is as though you have diverted the pressure right past him.

Of course, the fact that all that focus on providing more sensory input will improve the quality and quantity of sensory information to his brain is an important secondary benefit—a positive double-whammy.

## Comfort Zone

I mentioned in the previous chapter that an uncomfortable driver will not be a quick driver. Most times, a car that exceeds the driver's comfort level will not result in the performance you expected. Your driver will always get more out of a car that he is confident in, than one that is fast but difficult to drive at the limit.

This goes back to adapting the car to suit your driver's style. Even though there are times when the car could be made faster with a particular setup change, to suit your driver's style and to keep him in his comfort zone, it may be best to do something different to the car.

It is important that you observe closely to see when your driver is in or out of his comfort zone. If he is outside that zone, no matter what is done to the car to make it better, the driver-car package will not perform better. In most cases, the package will perform worse, even if the car is better. That is the time to dial the car back to within your driver's comfort zone, rebuild his confidence, then begin again to push his comfort zone envelope.

## Self-Discipline and Details

Perhaps this is more an observation than useful information for you, but through the years I have noticed a remarkable correlation between the attention a driver pays to his safety equipment (helmet, suit, etc.), and his abilities on the track. It is a rare driver who does well on the track, but does not take almost fanatical care of his equipment.

The reason is self-discipline and attention to details. If a driver does not take care of his equipment and himself, he probably will not pay enough attention to the details on the track.

Does that mean that if your driver is a slob you should dump him immediately? Not necessarily. But you may want to educate him on the value of the details. This applies equally whether he is off the track or on it. In fact, maybe more. The career of a race driver is all about self-discipline and attention to details.

## Fear

Not surprisingly, fear is part of a race driver's psyche, but maybe not in the way many people would imagine. Fear of injury or death is not a part of a good driver's program. If it is part of your driver's, he will not be a winner, for successful drivers have an ability to see injury or death as something that can only happen to others. Call that naïve, but it is a fact.

I'm not saying that good race drivers never have fear. In fact, if a driver ever says he has never been afraid in a race car, either he is not going fast enough or he is lying. Every driver has some level of fear, although I prefer to see it as his personal sense of self-preservation. Without that, he would crash at every corner. The biggest difference between all-out fear and self-preservation is that fear tends to make a person freeze up to some extent. It certainly creates anxiety and tension, which we know hurts a driver's performance. Self-preservation, on the other hand, just provides limits.

In my experience, fear of damage to the race car (and the financial repercussions of that), and fear of embarrassment are the two biggest fears that restrict the performance of drivers. In other words, fear of failure. Fear of failure is a much bigger factor than fear of injury or death with most race drivers.

So how do you deal with your driver's fear of failure? In terms of the fear of damaging the race car, you could arrange for a budget the size of a small country's gross national product, like some Formula One teams do, although that is probably unrealistic.

Instead, it comes back to what I talked about at the beginning of this chapter: keeping him focused on his own performance. You could tell your driver not to worry about damaging the car, or about the result or what anyone thinks or says about him, but you know that doesn't work. Reminding and refocusing your driver on what is important is the key to dealing with his fears, along with recognizing that his fears are real and justifiable.

In the previous chapter I mentioned that when a person tries to make the same error that is causing them problems, they become truly aware of the root cause of the problem, therefore allowing the person to cure it. That obviously means being unafraid of making errors, which is not comfortable for some people. Many drivers have been brought up with the attitude that any type of mistake is a bad thing, something to be avoided at all costs. This is a true shame, as mistakes are really just error-signals that lead a person in the direction toward perfection.

Now, I know what you are thinking: errors of any type in racing are going to be costly, so a driver has to avoid them at any cost. The ironic thing is that the more your driver tries to avoid them, the more likely it is for him to make them. It is a little like the Richard Petty approach to driving on an oval track: the closer you run to the walls, the less likely it is that you are going to hit them, and the less it will hurt when you do. The more a person avoids failure, the more likely it is to happen.

When your driver begins to see errors and not winning—"failures"—simply as guidance toward his goals, much, if not all the pressure will be removed.

## Beliefs

One of the traits of a true champion is his belief in himself. I have never heard a champion driver talk about other drivers with any sense of awe. But I have heard many drivers talk this way about other drivers. Of course, these drivers never become champions until their beliefs about themselves and others change.

Particularly when a driver is new to a series, it is easy for him to look up to the drivers who have been winning there. Some drivers actually place these winners on a pedestal, having a hard time believing they even belong on the same track. What do you suppose the chances are of a driver with this mindset beating the established stars? Slim to none—at best!

If your driver has anything other than a total belief that he is there to win every race, and that the other drivers on the track don't belong on his track, it is doubtful he will win often. The list of new, young drivers who have come into a series with a total belief that they are better than everyone else is short, but impressive. It is a list primarily made up of superstar drivers.

Let me remind you that there is a big difference between your driver's beliefs and his ego. If he goes around telling you and the world just how good he is, I would suspect that is more his ego talking than his belief system. But if he has that quiet confidence about him, look out!

If your driver begins to talk about other drivers with the slightest hint of awe, nip that in the bud. Often, referring to other drivers by their car number takes away some of the mystique about the drivers' abilities. It also takes the personality out of the equation. Every time your driver talks about another driver, have him refer to him by his car number.

You need to learn to recognize what your driver's beliefs are saying, and help him change them for the better if necessary, for his belief system may be the single most important factor limiting his performance.

# Chapter 11

# Driver Engineer

So now you are a driver engineer. Be careful! Never forget that being a driver engineer does not mean you are an expert, someone who can go around telling your driver how to drive. It may be tempting with all your newfound knowledge to take on the role of a teacher or instructor. Never lose sight of what your true role is: someone to bring out the best in your driver. Please use the information in this book for good, not evil!

### SPEED SECRET #34
### Coach your driver, but never instruct him.

Having provided this information, I think it's only fair to discuss the use of a professional coach—a professional driver engineer. While you will be much more capable of assisting your driver by applying the information in this book, I hope you begin to realize just how involved and difficult it can be to bring out the best in a race driver. I hope you understand the value of a professional coach who lives and breathes the techniques and strategies presented here.

Taking the information in this book and expecting to coach at the same level as a professional coach who works with drivers year-round is like expecting to read a book on driving technique and then immediately becoming a professional driver. Or reading a book on brain surgery and then performing an operation. Practical application and practice is a critical component to the success of working with a driver.

*The goal is simple: Do whatever it takes to help your driver perform at his maximum—and then raise the bar. If that means bringing someone else into the team, that's what a driver engineer does.* Kent Regan

While I truly believe you are now better prepared to assist your driver, a professional driver coach is just that—a pro. If a "coach" does this only when he is not racing himself, using the coaching job to keep him at the track and near his next ride, he is not a professional coach. A professional coach has chosen this as his career, not something he does while looking for a ride. A professional coach is trained in coaching techniques, and uses them on a regular basis. Like a race driver who drives a few times a year, versus one who drives every week, a professional coach who works with many drivers will always have an advantage.

As mentioned in the introduction, part of your job is to do whatever it takes to ensure your driver performs at his best, even if that means bringing in the services of a professional coach, or sending him to some form of driver development program. You must recognize whether you have the time and abilities or can be detached enough to do a great job of engineering your driver.

## SPEED SECRET #35
### *Do whatever it takes to improve your driver's performance.*

The bottom line is your driver's car will rarely win a race if your driver does not drive it to its maximum potential. Your team will not win often if your driver does not perform at his peak. No matter how much natural talent he has, your driver will only become a superstar by continually improving.

It is doubtful you can *teach* him to get the most out of the car, to perform at his peak, and to continually get better and better. But you can help him, guide him, tune him, *engineer* him to do that. Your ability to affect your driver's performance, in a positive way, may be the most difficult and challenging part of racing. And yet, it will undoubtedly be the most rewarding.

# Speed Secrets

*#1 The car will only perform as well as the driver who drives it.*

*#2 Engineering your driver does not mean telling him how to drive.*

*#3 The goal is to ensure your driver never makes the same mistake twice, or has to learn the same thing twice.*

*#4 Help your driver focus on his performance, and the results will look after themselves.*

*#5 Improve your driver's sensory input and he will drive better.*

*#6 Driving must be a programmed or habitual act—something done without "thinking."*

*#7 Everything, and everyone, affects your driver's programming. Use that to his and your advantage.*

*#8 The driver's beliefs about himself are the biggest limitations to his performance—and you can influence those beliefs.*

*#9 The more quality information your driver has, the better his on-track decisions will be.*

*#10 Provide your driver with something to focus on.*

*#11 Awareness is the key to improving*

*#12 If your driver is unable to do something, he's missing either mental image or awareness.*

*#13 Draw the answer out of your driver, rather than drill it into him.*

*#14 A learning plateau is the sign of an opportunity for improvement.*

*#15 Ask awareness-building questions—and then ask more.*

*#16 Use sensory input sessions on a regular basis to improve your driver's performance.*

*#17 Quantity and quality sensory input will lead to smaller errors.*

*#18 Provide your driver with the opportunity to do mental programming.*

*#19 Ensure your driver does his pre-drive ritual, including cross crawls and lazy 8s.*

*#20 Control your driver's focus—keep it on his performance.*

*#21 Build both your and your driver's awareness by observing.*

*#22 Ensure your driver has no more than three very specific objectives each time he heads onto the track.*

*#23 Your driver should keep notes on every aspect of his driving.*

*#24 Know when to teach, when to coach, when to motivate, and when to engineer your driver.*

*#25 Prioritize your driver's focus on the most important corners.*

*#26 Drive the car at the limit, and the line will take care of itself.*

*#27 Skid pad training should be mandatory for your driver.*

*#28 Drivers do what they do most often because the car "told" them to.*

*#29 The driver engineer may need to play facilitator to enhance communications between driver and team.*

*#30 Encourage and build team energy.*

*#31 Use data acquisition to enhance and confirm your driver's feedback.*

*#32 Use testing to develop the driver as much as to develop the car.*

*#33 Remove expectations by focusing on the possibilities.*

*#34 Coach your driver, but never instruct him.*

*#35 Do whatever it takes to improve your driver's performance.*

# *Recommended Reading*

- *Coaching For Performance*, John Whitmore

- *Drive To Win*, Carroll Smith

- *Extraordinary Golf*, Fred Shoemaker

- *Flow*, Mihaly Csikszentmihalyi

- *Jackie Stewart's Principles of Performance Driving*, Jackie Stewart

- *The Inner Game of Tennis*, Timothy Gallwey

- *Sacred Hoops*, Phil Jackson and Hugh Delehanty

- *Smart Moves*, Carla Hannaford

- *Speed Secrets: Professional Race Driving Techniques*, Ross Bentley

- *Speed Secrets 2: More Professional Race Driving Techniques*, Ross Bentley

- *Speed Secrets 3: Inner Speed Secrets*, Ross Bentley and Ronn Langford

# *About the Author*

Ross Bentley's goal is for race driver coaches to become as accepted as coaches in other sports. He has spent the past five years working toward that goal, and will not quit until people within motorsport appreciate the true value of coaches. He envisions the day when drivers on the tops of podiums at Formula One, Indy car, and NASCAR races recognize the contribution of their coaches along with the rest of the team. He sees the day when every pro race driver has a coach, just like any pro athlete does.

Ross has been instructing and coaching race drivers of all levels for the past 25 years. While he has worked with drivers at the highest levels of professional racing, he has a passion for helping young drivers begin their careers. He gets a real kick out of helping drivers take their performance, on and off the track, to an all-new level. He gets energized when coaching others to do the same, as proven by his team of Speed Secrets coaches.

While Ross has raced and won in virtually everything from Formula Fords to Indy Cars, from Showroom Stock to Prototype Sports cars, he does not see coaching as "second to driving." To him, coaching is a profession, one just as challenging and rewarding as race driving itself.

From his office in Redmond, Washington, and while traveling around the world, he continues to race sports cars, coach drivers, coach coaches, coach race team members, and change the way the motorsport world views coaches.

You can contact Ross at info@speed-secrets.com.

# Index

## ACCELERATE YOUR POTENTIAL WITH SPEED SECRETS

In addition to our collection of Speed Secrets books, we've been helping drivers and race teams all over the world accelerate their potential and develop the skills necessary to get their racing to the next level. We offer a comprehensive collection of resources geared to assist you in becoming a more complete driver and building your competitive advantage – on and off the track. Here's how we can help:

### DRIVER DEVELOPMENT CAMPS AND CLINICS

Our unique camps combine break-through coaching strategies, skills development, the most complete motorsports curriculum available plus a ton of track time.

### COACHING SERVICES

Our Speed Secrets Certified coaches have worked with drivers from club racers right up to CART and they can provide you with insights and training on how to improve your skills on the track. Our coaches can work with you on a complete driver development program or just help you maximize a race weekend.

### SEMINARS AND WORKSHOPS

Our seminars and workshops are a must for any driver, engineer or team owner who is serious about improving. These informative sessions cover a wide range of topics from Inner Speed Secrets techniques to racecraft, to engineering the driver as well as marketing and sponsorship.

For further information on the complete range of Speed Secrets Driver Development Services call us toll free at 1-877-773-3310 or visit us online at www.speedsecrets.com

### ➔ SPECIAL OFFER for SPEED SECRETS 4 readers.

To receive access to special offers and promotions please visit our website www.speedsecrets.com/ss4

## Other MBI Publishing Company titles of interest:

**Speed Secrets:
Professional Race
Driving Techniques**
ISBN 0-7603-0518-8

**Speed Secrets 2:
More Professional Race
Driving Techniques**
ISBN 0-7603-1510-8

**Speed Secrets 3:
Inner Speed Secrets**
ISBN 0-7603-0834-9

**Bob Bondurant on
Race Kart Driving**
ISBN 0-7603-1076-9

**Stock Car Driving
Techniques**
ISBN 0-7603-0958-2

**High-Performance
Handling Handbook**
ISBN 0-7603-0948-5

**Porsche
High-Performance
Driving Handbook**
ISBN 0-8793-8849-8

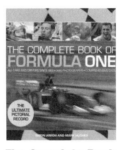

**The Complete Book
of Formula One**
ISBN 0-7603-1688-0

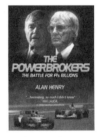

**The Powerbrokers**
ISBN 0-7603-1650-3

**Find us on the internet at www.motorbooks.com 1-800-826-6600**